NE
BEGINNINGS

Anne Nolan

With John Stephenson

ISBN: 978-1-915657-10-7

MMXXIV

A CIP catalogue record for this is available from the British Library

Published by
Pressman House Publishing Ltd.
Boston, Lincs, PE20 3BT, England
Tel: +44 (0) 1296695588

This book is dedicated to my daughters Amy and Alex, and to my grandchildren Vinny, Ryder and Nevaeh for making my life so happy and complete.

Acknowledgements

Thank you to Marc Nixon for all your unselfish hard work and help in getting me started with this, my second autobiography.

To Julian Nolan, for persuading me to continue writing the book and for your endless hard work helping me to get back into finishing it.

To John Stephenson at Pressman House for your patience, advice and assistance.

To my family, especially my daughters, Amy and Alex, and friends, especially Jacqui Bloom and Adam Nolan, for helping me with times and dates of various episodes in my life and supplying endless photos and encouragement.

Contents

Chapter

Prologue

As I stood behind the red velvet curtain that draped across the stage on one of the world's most luxurious ships, I could feel my hand clench to the microphone as a sense of sheer apprehension pulsated through my body.

This would be the very first time that I had performed alongside my sisters on a professional occasion since the family fall out that dominated the press. We were to be performing our biggest-selling hit, 'I'm In the Mood For Dancing' in front of a jampacked theatre, as a part of our reality TV series, *The Nolans Go Cruising*. If you had told me that I would be reunited alongside my sisters a decade before, I probably would've laughed, as this came at the time in 2009, when Maureen, Linda, Coleen and Bernie went on tour to celebrate the 30th anniversary of 'I'm In the Mood For Dancing' across the UK and Ireland, playing to massive arenas and theatres that left me excluded.

This was the infamous reunion tour that divided the family and left a ripple effect that hindered many relationships that would follow us for years to come and would remain a sore subject to this day, that we do not talk about. I couldn't have imagined in 2009 that I'd be sitting here again writing my second autobiography; little did we know then how much little time we had left with my beautiful little sister, Bernie, who would be taken from us at such a young age after fighting with cancer which has cursed our family.

Thankfully, before Bernie's death, Denise and I had written to our sisters asking for a reconciliation which Maureen and Bernie agreed to immediately. Coleen and Linda took a little bit longer to reply. Some relationships needed more time to heal than others; we're a big family with lots of personalities and views. Like every family there are some members closer to each other than others. In this book I will tell you about my life since my first autobiography *Anne's Song* was released and, as I mentioned before, the breakdown and reconnection of the family dynamic, and tell you what it was like working with my sisters again on our hit TV series *The Nolans Go Cruising.*

The first draft of this book was written in 2018 and I have kept it in a drawer buried beneath birthday cards and other pieces of stationery that mingle in my little desk at home in Blackpool. Shortly after I finished writing the book, I decided that I would not release it, in fear that there would be another family fall out and I did not want the release of this book to hinder my reconnected relationships with my sisters.

Yes, what happened with the family fall out was a traumatic time and it is a topic that is not broached when we are all together, because underneath it all there is no reason to look back; we should only look forward. If I had released the book back then, I wouldn't be able to tell you about the amazing things I've done since then and some of the heartaches I've endured as well, because that's life. I decided to write this book after enduring a year's programme of third stage breast cancer treatment – when my life was threatened, I asked myself what do I want to be remembered for? The answer is that I want people to know how happy I am now in my life and how I want to spend the rest of my days on this glorious place.

Now, sit back relax and enjoy my story.

Nolan Family Tree

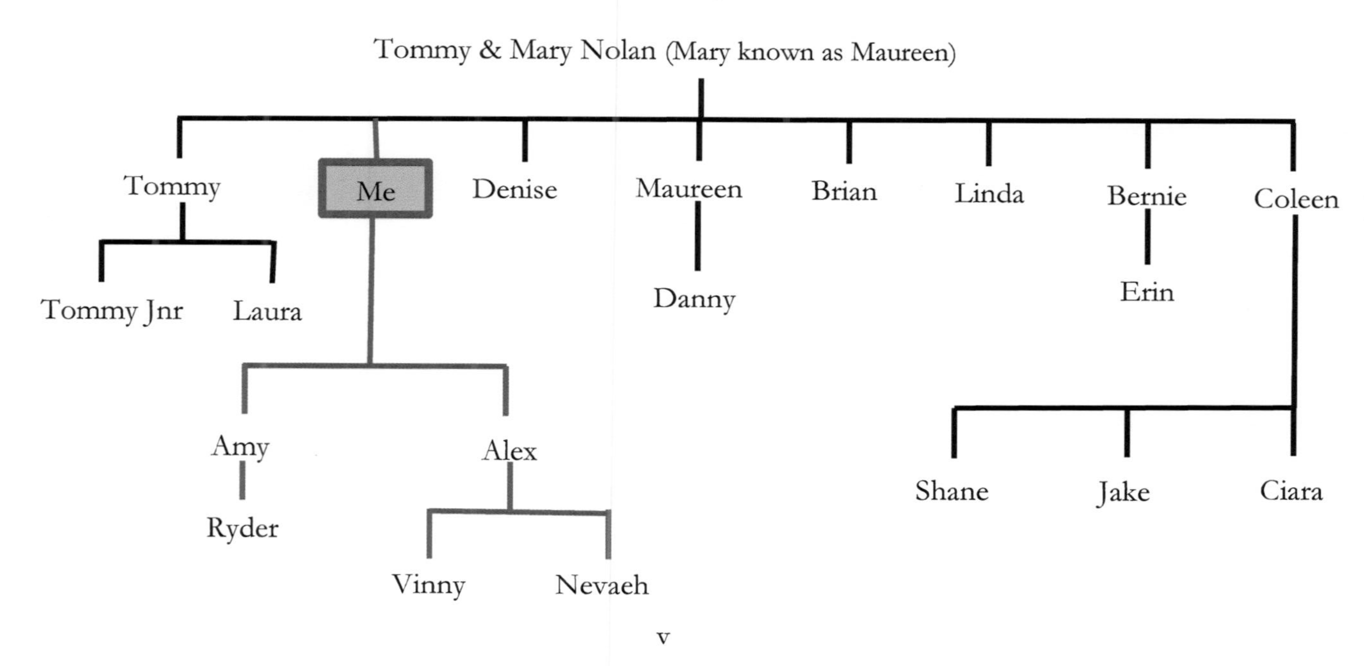

Chapter 1

Is This the Beginning of the End?

I released my autobiography *Anne's Song* in 2008 after the death of my parents because I didn't want them to have to deal with the revelations in the book.

I was surprised by its success and was invited to lots of radio stations, magazines and newspapers. I even went home to Ireland to promote the book on Irish TV. It climbed the book chart, and I was told it reached no 3 in the Sunday Times Book chart, which I believe is quite a prestigious chart, and for a day or so made it to the number-one spot on the Amazon chart. Not bad for a girl from the Raheny council estate in Dublin.

I had been prepared to travel to promote the book, but I had no idea how much travelling it entailed. It was different to anything that I had ever done before. Even if you are in panto in a town far away from home you make friends with the cast really quickly. Everyone is in the same boat, so you spend your free time with them. When you are promoting a book, you are on your own. I trailed up and down the UK and made a trip home to Ireland as part of the promotion. I also joined the queen of daytime TV, Lorraine Kelly, in the studio for an interview on ITV. If you are a really successful author, you might have a team to accompany you. In my case I was largely alone. This gave me plenty of time to assess the family situation.

I was happy with the content of the book and the positive reviews but, given the explosive nature of the book, I was right to expect a backlash. To go public that I had been a victim of childhood sexual abuse by my father was going to be hard for some people to take. I countered that by saying that I was going to be telling everything that had happened in my life, both good and bad. Largely, it had been a fantastic life as I had met lots of my heroes and seen most of the world by the time I was twenty-five.

When the book's contents became public it was met with mixed feelings by my wider family. Prior to its release, I hadn't informed some of the more distant relatives of the full story so I didn't know what their reaction would be. Some of my family members were not happy at me disclosing that my dad had sexually abused me, or, for that matter, that he had been a heavy drinker and had often been violent. A couple of my dad's family met the book with outright hostility. His younger sister would not believe, or didn't want to believe, what I had written, and she never spoke to me again.

His older sister met with me in Blackpool to discuss what I had written, and she said it was very difficult for her to believe it but on the other hand she didn't disbelieve it either. I understood both of their reactions as they were natural. I would find it very hard to believe something like that about someone I loved but I knew the truth and that was enough for me. It wasn't only I who had the monopoly on revealing shocking truths about our family history. In my sister's autobiography's many stories have been revealed.

Well, a lot has happened since my first autobiography was published; my life didn't end in 2008 and I still have a life and a story to tell. So much of it has been fabulous, like becoming a grandparent, recording my own album, filming three record-breaking series with my sisters and then the awful things involved when a family falls out making the national press. However, the worst thing of all was losing a sister to cancer and, for the second time, fighting for my life against the vile disease.

Yes, now as I write this book, I ask myself is it necessary to talk about The Nolan's' 30th Anniversary Reunion Tour that I was excluded from, should I bring it up? Am I reopening old wounds? Will this book hinder my relationship with my sisters again? I don't know for certain, but it is a period of my life that caused a great deal of pain. I need to be honest and transparent and explain my side of the events that unfolded.

Life was OK after the release of my first book. People think that when you write a book you have tons of money, but it isn't really like that unless you are the likes of Jackie Collins or JK Rowling; I still had to work after my book. How show business works, you could be the hottest thing in town one minute and the next, you're phoning around looking for work. So, things were pretty bleak after the huge success of my book.

I was offered touring roles around the country in fun musicals. However, being a single mum of two daughters and a golden retriever and staying in my aunty's house the money offers were never substantial enough. Fun as it may sound these shows are often rehearsed for two weeks and then you're living out of a suitcase for six months and staying in Premier Inns or Travelodges up and down the country. I couldn't leave my girls with my aunty for that amount of time as, by now, her health was starting to decline and, frankly, they are not her responsibly. That is not to say that Aunty Teresa wouldn't have looked after the girls. At the end of the day, she gave us everything when we lost our home as a result of my marriage breakdown.

My sisters by now were all busy working on their own projects and we just got on normally. Denise was still a regular on the West End & cruise ship scene, Maureen was playing the lead of Mrs Johnston in *Blood Brothers* on the West End; poor Linda was learning to cope following the death of her beloved husband, Brian, who sadly passed away the year before. Bernie's solo career was flourishing with a sell-out summer season in Blackpool's Opera House and a studio album, *All By Myself* while Coleen was going from strength to strength after signing to a new London talent agency that catapulted her into becoming one of the country's most loved TV personalities.

Coleen was working an awful lot in London, where they film *Loose Women*, she would often spend 3-4 days per week working and be back home for the remainder with her family.

One day we were walking through the park when she asked me if I knew any of Amy or Alex's friends who would be interested in working a few hours a day looking after her daughter, Ciara, after school and doing some light cleaning and perhaps prepare dinner. I immediately jumped at the opportunity, saying, "I'll do it." Coleen later admitted that she didn't want to insult me by asking if I'd take Ciara and be employed by her younger sister, but I was so relieved. This meant I'd be less than ten minutes from home, keep an eye on my own girls and spend time with my gorgeous six-year-old niece, Ciara.

I loved looking after Ciara, she was such a beautiful little girl and I never had any trouble with her. On the days when I was around at Coleen's after school I'd make lunch, help Ciara with her homework and just tidy around the house. I would love to say that everything was smooth sailing, but it wasn't.

Sometimes during the day Ray would be home as he is a musician. He would often arrive home late at night so, when we got back to the house after school, we would sneak through the front door quietly until we got into the kitchen at the back of the house in case Ray was still sleeping. There we could do her homework and make dinner.

Ray and I got on well and chatted about work and showbiz and stuff like that. However, on one particular occasion there was a heated exchange that manifested into a bigger problem than it needed to be.

One day after collecting Ciara on the school run, I pulled up in the car outside the house and noticed that Ray's car was parked outside. We went into the house as usual and I made Ciara a quick snack before she tackled her homework. I was in the lounge with Ray telling him that Amy had decided to call it a day with the girl band she had formed, as work had dried up in the town. None of them drove yet, which made it difficult for them to get to gigs elsewhere. When the summer season ends in Blackpool, the town is virtually abandoned and nearly impossible to secure a gig.

Ray then lifted his head and said, "I think both your girls are talented but, in the end, they can't be arsed can they?"

I jumped to the defence of my girls, as any mother would, saying they were talented but they didn't really want to be in show business so they would use their talents elsewhere as they are both very hard-working girls. There were other comments made but I really didn't want to argue with him because I didn't want Ciara to hear so I just left him to his own devices.

As I finished off cleaning the house and approached the office door, there was a sharp sense of tension in the air as I bobbed my head round the door and said, "OK, I'll see you tomorrow."

Ray was at his computer and turned around in one of those office chairs and told me that I wasn't to bother coming back the next day.

I was dumbfounded. I replied, "OK, that's alright," not wanting him to see how hurt I was. I got back into my car and when I got home phoned Coleen to explain what had happened. I explained that I would still have Ciara around at mine, as I thought that it would all blow over in a couple of days and it would be fine.

However, it didn't turn out that way. Over the coming days things went from bad to ugly with our relationship. One regret in all of this is that I wish I could have nipped it in the bud with Ray and moved on. In a family like ours, there are so many different characters and personalities and when other family members caught wind of what had happened, they also voiced their opinions. Denise and Aunty, in particular, and they made it clear to Coleen they thought Ray was out of order for firing me at a time in my life when life wasn't easy.

Immediately this caused a divide in the family putting us in two different camps, with some members not getting involved and others speaking their mind. From then on it caused another crack in the family feud, and in the coming months communications between Coleen and Ray and me, Aunty and Denise began to get more and more quiet.

When one door closes, another opens. I wasn't looking after Ciara anymore and got a full-time job with the Civil Service.

It wasn't easy trying to find a job at the age I was with little or no experience in anything but show business but one advisor from the Job Centre had been really helpful and got me prepared for a possible job at the Insolvency Service as an Administrative Assistant. I was successful with my application and commenced working full time. It was a permanent position with the Civil Service complete with a pension scheme so I decided to put show business, as a full-time career, on the back burner for a while.

Don't get me wrong, I missed it terribly. It is difficult to get it out of your blood when you have been doing it most of your life. Opportunities were still coming my way that enabled me to enjoy a show business life as well as a regular one.

The Hilton Hotel in Blackpool, for example, had an opening on Saturday nights for the summer of 2007 where I would appear in cabaret doing two sets a night. The money was not fantastic at just £200 a night, but it did supplement my day job earnings and it gave me my fix of the showbiz drug. With so much upset over the whole of the year, I couldn't help but wonder if there would be a time when things would return to as they used to be.

Sometime later Coleen announced that she and Ray were going to get married at a castle just outside Leeds and she had asked Amy and Alex to be two of her bridesmaids. The wedding was going to be quite a grand occasion. Although I was invited, Denise and Aunty were not, so I declined. Looking back now it is a real shame but at the time, our relationships were not in the best of shapes.

On the day of Coleen and Ray's wedding we rented a barge from a friend and spent the day up and down the Lancaster ship canal. We had a lovely time as we laughed, sang, drank wine and it took our minds off everything else.

From left: Trudy Woolford (deceased), Denise, Auntie Teresa, Me, Celia Garside on the Lancaster Canal during the weekend away.

Chapter 2

Mending Bridges

2007

Just two weeks after the wedding, I was on my travels as a solo entertainer. This time I was to visit Spain. I had been booked to appear in concert at a theatre in the beautiful town of Nerja. My former manager, Marc, lived in Spain at the time with his partner Sandy and had arranged for me to do my very own solo concert. Everything was sorted out at his end, so all I had to do was get on a plane and get to Malaga. My friend Adam Nolan (no relation), who is also my hairdresser, travelled with me for a little break in the sun and to keep me company on the plane. He also ended up doing my sound for the show as there was no sound engineer to be found when we got there.

I performed The Nolan's back catalogue, some diva hits, and a highlight of mine was performing a duet with Frank Sinatra, who was shown in a film on a gigantic screen behind me in the jam-packed Spanish theatre. The music for the film was done by Rick Coates and thanks to Adam behind the controls.

After the show we retired to Marc and Sandy's restaurant for an after-show party. The show had been a big success and I was really glad I did it. We flew home two days later after a very successful and enjoyable few days and looking forward to Christmas.

Our whole family love Christmas. We have always tried to spend the actual day together. That is not an easy task. Often, we are in pantomimes very far away from each other. Whenever we are in panto we finish on Christmas Eve and are back at the theatre on Boxing Day. If you are away doing panto in somewhere like Torquay or Glasgow, it is a real slog to get home for one day. We have even had to go back to wherever it is we are appearing after dinner on Christmas Day and drive for hours to be ready for work for a matinee performance the next day.

On Christmas Day we had dinner at Denise and Tom's house, where afterwards we all sang together around the table. After that we opened presents and had a party. It was fabulous. Bernie turned up with her husband Steve and their daughter Erin. They brought a gorgeous puppy with them called Dexter which they had bought for Erin. That year I hadn't done panto and, to be honest, I am glad that I had turned down the offer. For the first time in years, I could spend the whole of the Christmas Season with my girls and the rest of my family.

The week in between Christmas and New Year brought further unhappiness for everyone. In the last week of 2007, my beloved mum became more ill and on 30th December, she passed away. This was a truly awful and painful release from Alzheimer's which she had endured for more than four years and which I wrote about in my first book. At her funeral at the Sacred Heart Church in Blackpool, I sang *Ave Maria,* adapted from Bach's prelude No1 in C major by Charles Gounod, which she had taught me to sing. It took so much concentration not to break down.

****

2008

In October 2008 we celebrated my youngest daughter Alex's twenty-first birthday. Alex and I had scoured Blackpool to find a suitable venue. It is never easy when you are planning a Nolan family party. For a start there is a timing issue. Usually, we are scattered about all over the place. To give credit to all my family, we have travelled crazy miles just to attend a family party so I knew everyone would make the effort to be there. Maureen had been constantly touring for several years, and for this, like so many times before, she would have to finish the show at ten thirty at night and then drive flat out to get to the party for the last hour or so. Only to get up early to get back to wherever for the next night's show.

As well as buying Alex a car, providing the catering and entertainment for the party, I had arranged to have a video made to celebrate twenty-one years of Alex's life. It was to be a surprise and was top secret. I got photographs that haven't seen the light of day for years. I had chosen a beautiful song by one of my favourite singers of all time, Barbra Streisand, to play in the background to the photographs. The song is a beautiful ballad about a mother protecting her child and the lyrics marked the occasion perfectly. The song includes the lines;

> *"If I could,*
> *I would help you make it through the hungry years*
> *But I know that I can never cry your tears*
> *But I would*
> *If I could"*

That song is rather special to me: the lyrics are perfect. Denise is like one of the paparazzi at every family occasion; you can't turn around without seeing her with a camcorder or a camera in your face. When she is actually doing the videoing and taking photos, we sometimes are a bit irritated but in later years we are always so grateful that she did it as we have some amazing photographic memories because of Denise as she has photographs and videos of everything.

At the arranged time we gathered everyone around and showed the video that my friend Adam and I had made. As the lovely tune played and the pictures came into view the whole family were sobbing. It was a joy to share the moment with everyone. The party cost a fortune, but it was worth every penny. We had a live band and a disco, and members of the family got up and sang too.

My ex-husband, Brian, turned up with his new wife. Our relationship had begun to heal. Over the years it had gone from hot to cold and back to hot again with varying shades of warm in between. When he came into the hotel with his wife, I thought it might be a good time to settle our differences. Later on, as the night was coming to an end, I said to him that I thought it was time that we should try and be friends and get along with each other. He had a new partner is his life, and I was trying to move on with mine and it was only natural that they attend occasions together which involved our children. In typical Nolan fashion people stayed at the hotel chatting and drinking until about six a.m. With the party over, things went straight back to normal very quickly.

2009

In early 2009 Alex called me to tell me she was expecting her first child. The baby was due in September and I was ecstatic. The news quickly spread through my family, and we all started buying bootees! As happens so often in our family, pregnancy seems contagious. Maureen told us a short time later that she too was to become a grandmother. Her son, Danny, and his girlfriend, Anne-Marie, were expecting a baby as well. Theirs would be due in November. Alex was planning to set up home with her long-term partner, Steve, before the baby was born.

She bloomed during her pregnancy and doctors were happy with her throughout the early stages. Then she was delivered a bombshell that floored us all. Scans had detected that her baby was suffering with gastroschisis which is quite rare. Without being overly technical it means that one or more of the intestines of the baby extend outside the developing body. They usually come from a hole next to the baby's belly button. There was no immediate risk, but doctors would closely monitor both mother and baby and she was placed under the care of St Mary's paediatric hospital in Manchester. I must add that the care they extended to Steve and Alex was nothing short of outstanding. They explained that her baby would need a major operation shortly after he was born and decided that Alex should book into the hospital to give birth at the predetermined date of September 8th. We had all talked about names for the new baby with me offering my favourite boy's names, which were all traditional and not at all like the ones they were suggesting. In the end they settled for Vinny Joe.

One of my sisters told me that Coleen was to be starring in *Dancing On Ice,* the hit ITV show and I was very proud of her. There are sixteen years between Coleen and me, and even though we were not on speaking terms I was delighted to see my baby sister doing so well on her own. At this time, we rarely saw each other as she bought a brand-new home in Wilmslow, Cheshire, about an hour and a bit from

Blackpool, so we never bumped into each other in my other sisters' houses or in the shops.

The list of contestants was a secret and speculation about who was taking part was all over the press. When the series aired, I made sure I never missed a show. I also spent a fortune on premium rate numbers calling to register votes to see her go through to the next round. When I heard she had been injured I was really worried. I knew she had an existing back problem and was frightened she might make it worse. I saw her make progress on the ice, but I knew she was not as accomplished as some of the other skaters. We are all fans of the reality TV show genre, and I would love to have a go at *Strictly Come Dancing*. I would never try *I'm A Celebrity Get Me Out of Here* because I am a very jumpy with creepy crawlies. You would think we would be used to them with some of the people we have met professionally!

Chapter 3

Not In the Mood Again?

2009

I was sitting at home on the sofa in early March flicking through the TV guide when I heard the ringtone from my phone, without hesitation I picked it up and it was Maureen on the end of the line. We chatted a few minutes about normal things like how my girls were doing. She had recently embarked on a UK tour of *Blood Brothers* playing the role of Mrs Johnstone. I asked how the tour was going and we chatted with ease. Maureen and I had been exceptionally close. We worked together since I was twelve and carried the torch for The Nolans as a duo for almost a decade before calling it a day in 2005. As the conversation carried on, she told me she had some news and that I probably wasn't going to like it.

I steeled myself and replied, "What is it, Maureen?" thinking it might be something to do with a family member.

She said, "We're going on tour." I felt the rush of anxiety ease from my body; however, little did I know moments later it would come back with a bang.

With a sigh of relief I responded, "Oh, OK… That's good."

She then stunned me by saying, "Well the thing is, we've already had meetings with the tour promoters and it's a really massive deal. It's to celebrate the 30th anniversary of 'I'm In the Mood For Dancing'. It could mean that we might never have to work again. They want us to play arenas and do an album."

She then went on to tell me that the record company only wanted the four sisters who had been in the act when we had our biggest successes and that I was not going to be included in the tour. It was then that I realised that they had already been in discussion with tour promoters and had several of these meetings without telling me. I sensed that something wasn't right.

I snapped down the phone at Maureen, "Well, thanks for telling me!" She explained that all the girls had backed me up. Maureen claimed that they had all pleaded with the record company executives, managers and tour promoters to let me be part of the reunion. She tried to take the sting out of the situation by telling me that all of them had agreed to put some money aside from any profits to make sure I wouldn't miss out completely. What Maureen was saying to me just didn't add up. I said something about it being OK and that I would get over it once I had processed things and got used to the idea.

As soon as I put the phone down, I could feel my stomach drop and felt an overwhelming sense of betrayal. My mind went into overdrive; I had dozens of questions rushing around my head. The whole thing had a terrible stench about it. The very fact that they had gone to meetings in London for talks at the highest level with the UK's biggest tour promoter, told me that this hadn't just happened overnight. Furthermore, as it was the anniversary of 'I'm In the Mood For Dancing', it was a real kick in the teeth as I had recorded and promoted the original record. Now, on its anniversary, I was not to be part of the party.

Even more galling was that, apart from two years when I left the act because I was about to give birth to Amy, I had never been out of the group. I had clocked up a whooping twenty-eight years from 1974-2005. For what it matters. Linda had left the act in 1983, so twenty-six years had passed without her being in the group. Coleen had left in 1993 and Bernie in 1994, leaving Maureen and myself carrying the torch for eleven years without the others. As I sat in the lounge now in front of a blank TV screen alone with my own thoughts, I started to process all of this. It began to dawn on me that there was no reason at all as far as I could see for me not to be part of the reunion tour. I was singing just as well as any of my sisters. My figure wasn't bad, and I didn't look like some craggy old woman. That obviously is a matter of opinion of course! I called some of my friends on the phone and they were all equally stunned. There had to be another reason behind this.

Over the years promoters, managers and record companies have promised us the world and then always fallen short of their promises. Even when we were at the height of our success, we were still being conned with big shots with pipe dreams.

My sisters and their manager, whom I spoke to on the phone, told me their reasons for me not being included in the tour but I didn't believe any of it and subsequently we fell out. Denise was horrified that I had not been included and was so supportive, which is something I will never forget. She and I did not speak to our four sisters for a long time.

In the months that followed, life went on without speaking to the foursome, until June 2009. Our musical director announced he was getting married and it was suggested that the sisters would sing at the ceremony. It is something our family have always done at weddings and christenings and so on, so we were only too happy to take part. We are singers after all!

In view of the falling out I was asked if there would be a problem singing with my sisters. I was clear in my response, I didn't have a problem singing with my sisters at all, especially as it was for our musical director and friend for many years. On several occasions we all went round to his house to practise, and we were all perfectly civil to each other. The wedding went without a hitch and we sat at the other end of the reception venue with each other.

I took a lot of comfort from my friends. My best friend of over six decades, Jacqui, was always at the end of the phone with kind words. She had a lot going on in her own life with her parents not in good health. She also had children of her own and a disabled brother to care for. Her love and support never wavered. She would jump in her car to come and see me or suggest that we go out for the day to take my mind off things. Work was something else I could throw myself into. It concentrated my mind and completely distracted me.

The tour was set for the autumn of 2009, and I couldn't escape the endless trail of publicity. I would switch on the radio first thing in the morning and there my sisters would be promoting the tour. I'd walk around Tesco and they'd be on the cover of countless magazines. Posters were draped around the town as they were playing in the Opera House in Blackpool, a venue we had played countless times and was almost like our second home. It was an overwhelming feeling of being left out, and I couldn't figure out why I was being excluded from this once-in-a-lifetime opportunity.

In the summer, to escape what was happening, I joined Tom and Denise in Spain for my beautiful cousin Val's marriage to her lovely man, Richard. Again, it was a wonderful day with a church wedding where Val's gorgeous daughter Lauren sang beautifully. Not just the Nolans sing, all our extended family have lovely voices. The reception was held at a beautiful beach side restaurant and after the wedding day we hired a car and explored all the lovely towns and villages far away from the resort. We stopped at little restaurants and ate traditional tapas lunches. We even found a place that Maureen and I had been to many years before with Brian and Maureen's then partner Pete Suddaby, who played football with Brian at Blackpool. We re-acquainted ourselves with the owner, who still happened to be there: a very handsome Spaniard whom I had a slow dance with while Denise took to the stage. After that, I too was up singing a love song. You see we can't help ourselves! Denise always says that when someone opens the fridge door and the light comes on, she goes into her act. I think we are all a little guilty of that.

That night was a blissful, balmy evening full of memory-making moments with sangria, great food and a smooch with a fine-looking restaurant owner. It was nice and a little romantic to dance in the open air, underneath the stars and the moonlight.

We had all decided to escape again from what was going on at home and treat ourselves to a well needed holiday after a traumatic few months and booked to go to Florida in October. It was at this time a young chap called Billy Walker got in touch. He was, and still is, a fabulous actor and singer. He wrote to me after hearing that I had been left out of my sister's tour to lend his support and he got me some really good work singing and doing interviews.

Before we went on holiday, he managed to get me an invitation that still, remains one of the highlights of my solo professional career. The organisation behind the Manchester Pride asked if I would take part in their main stage event on August Bank Holiday.

I was, frankly, terrified. This is one of the biggest Gay Pride events in the world. Up to 40,000 buy an entry wristband every day. Topping the bill was Peter Andre, with loads more well-known names.

The controversial Nolans tour hadn't kicked off yet so this was an opportunity to showcase my capability. Some of the wounds had started to heal, I did feel that my confidence had taken a knock. As I said earlier, it wasn't the fact that I doubted my ability; it was that I had been told that I *wasn't wanted.* Nagging doubts were swirling around my head. As the day drew nearer, I had to choose my set. I wanted my act to mean something to the audience. The gay crowds always loved a party song, but they also love a torch song. Someone suggested I have a crack at 'I Am What I Am' which I wasn't sure about. I knew it had been a big hit with the gay community years ago, but what if the audience that day were all twenty-one years old? Would they be standing there saying, "What the hell is this song? Who is that middle-aged woman singing this rubbish?"

When you are part of such a diverse line-up there is no way that you can know what they are all into. I had a track prepared with a really modern dance beat. It started really soft and quiet and then exploded into a disco track. My gay friends told me it was really camp.

I had nothing to go on except what they told me would work.

In the end I decided to sing the following: 'Footloose', 'Man, I Feel Like a Woman', 'Hot Stuff', 'You Don't Have To Say You Love Me' and then do a false tab closing number, the disco version of 'I am What I Am' before coming back with the inevitable 'In The Mood For Dancing. I rehearsed until I was shattered.

I was so determined to get it right. My spot would be twenty minutes, which, on the face of it, was fantastic. If it went well then it was going to flash by in a heartbeat. If it didn't, it would seem like an eternity, but what the hell, it was only twenty minutes, so it was a win-win situation.

What's more, I knew that the press would certainly be there watching my first performance without my sisters since their tour. I needed this to go well to prove to them I was well worth being included in their tour.

I was told that there would be up to 20,000 people in the audience. What I didn't know is that the Manchester Pride is the only event of its kind that has consistently made money for charity. The year before it made over £120,000 for charity, including HIV awareness and treatment. This was a really big deal, and I was so excited to be a part of it.

Billy sorted out everything for the Pride gig, hotel, sound, travelling, etc. and my friend Stacey did my hair and make-up. I drove over to the event relieved that they had booked me an overnight hotel stay. I was able to relax and have my hair and make-up done and a glass of wine to steady my nerves. As time drew closer, nerves became more evident, but I knew I wanted to do it more than anything.

Security was tight. They even took my handbag away from me saying I could have it back as I left. The backstage area was pretty grotty, and it was surrounded by large fences. Portaloos stood in a row looking as uninviting as they could be. They stank, and I was determined not to use one. In between the eight-foot-high fence panels were small gaps which I could peep through and see the audience. If that didn't induce panic – nothing would. All the artistes were ushered into a marquee with a bar and green room area which was really nice. We were at the back of the square facing the stage. I could see thousands of people in front of me.

Before I went on, I watched a Madonna tribute act and a singer called Lonnie Gordon who had a huge hit with the song 'Happening All Over Again'. I know both Madonna and Lonnie Gordon are massive gay icons so I was still unsure how I would go down. I had chosen a red sequinned outfit with skin-tight leggings. My friends were telling me that I looked great, which helped a lot. Natasha Hamilton from Atomic Kitten was in the green room and organisers came and took her to the holding area at the side of the stage. Then the nerves really kicked in.

I was following Natasha Hamilton, as she took to the stage someone came and I headed to the holding area. I was not allowed to take anyone with me. I could see Natasha on stage. She was singing her heart out. I hoped I would do as well as she did.

The stage area was an articulated lorry with the side opened up. It had lots of flashing lights, speakers and monitors. There was even a sign language translator at the side. Because there are so many acts on stage, one after the other, there's no time for any rehearsals. I had already had a very brief chat with the sound man about the levels I wanted and how much reverb to use. In all the years I had been on stage, I had never done something so off the cuff in front of such a large audience. They all seemed so young and trendy as well. As I waited to go on my heart was thumping. I am usually a little nervous, that is good as it helps with your performance but the nerves I had now were off the scale. I was scared I might drop the microphone or say I couldn't go on at the last minute. I had visions of the crew pushing me up the steps to the stage!

Natasha's spot finished in what seemed like a couple of minutes. Before I knew it, a man had taken my hand and was leading me up the stairs to a little box at the side of the stage area. I could see the crowd and I thought my legs were going to give way.

There had been a lot of press interest in the tour and the fall out. I could see a full press pack at the front of the stage in a separate press area, I felt that all of their eyes were on me and it really concentrated my mind. Two men took to the centre of the stage and introduced me I still remember the intro that the compere announced.

"There have been hundreds of girl groups over the years. Few, if any, can claim to have had the success or the enduring appeal of the group that our next guest was a member of.

"With twenty-five million record sales and more sales in Japan than the Beatles, would you please welcome, from the Nolans… ANNE NOLAN!"

I heard the intro to 'Footloose' and I was on. As soon as I got on stage any nerves I had quickly vanished. The crowd were incredible. They were cheering and singing along to every word. I sang my choice of songs ending with the specially prepared 'I am What I Am'. At one point I felt my confidence soar and I said to the audience:

"I think I am older that a lot of your grandmothers!" It sounds really cheesy to say it, but I could feel the goodwill and love coming over me in waves. I was smiling and strutting my stuff on that stage watching these young people having the best time. The thing is, I was having an even better time! Some were dressed in drag from their march on the parade earlier that day; some wore leather shorts and harnesses, and some wore rainbow-coloured fun wigs. They blew whistles and waved flags and banners. To me it felt like I was the headline act at Glastonbury. Before I knew it, my set was over. Yet I still hadn't sung our signature song. I had walked off the stage and waited in the box at the side.

The compere shouted at the crowd: "You want some more?"

They cheered back – "YES!"

As they cheered, I heard the intro to my encore.

I knew that the crowd would want to hear 'I'm In the Mood for Dancing' and so I had deliberately chosen to do it as an encore. When it came thundering over the PA, the audience went crazy. It was such an emotional experience, that when I came off stage I was shaking and a little tearful. Think a lot of it was adrenaline, which is normal but there was something else. Maybe it was a validation that I *was* good enough. If that record company really did have those reservations, then they were wrong. I had just done a performance in front of more than twenty thousand people watching. I made my way to the bar and bought everyone in our group a drink.

When I came back from the bar, I was told that one of the artistes in the green room, a singer from a reality show had made her way to our group and sneered, "Is she the one who was a bitch to her sisters?"

Stacey, the girl who had done my make-up, snapped, "No! It's other people who have been bitches to her."

This particular artiste just slunk away and said something about being sorry that she had got it wrong. She had been one of the first to come over to me and say how fantastic I was. I hadn't heard the story of her being vile at that time and thought how lovely she was. Little did I know what she had really been saying while I was on stage. Some people are just so two faced.

Peter Andre was the top of the bill that day. I am sure he is a lovely man. I can't say for sure because I never met him. I've always liked him as an artist and his persona. He always comes across as so personable. On that day though no one had a chance to meet him. He was brought in, surrounded by security people and managers. He waited in the holding area at the side of the stage. He was having a microphone fitted, about thirty feet from where I was standing, trying to exit the venue.

The security people wouldn't let me out until he was on stage, which I thought was ridiculous.

I said, "I want to get out, I have a car ticket about to expire. What do you think I am going to do to him?"

The security people just stood there with their arms folded and shook their heads.

I walked past them and tried the gate, but it was locked, which made me look a bit daft.

The main man, who was about six foot seven, said, "Sorry, I can't let you out until Mr Andre is on stage."

I am sure this rule was something Peter Andre had not insisted on. I doubt he was bothered in the slightest that fellow entertainers were in reach of him.

Personally, I couldn't see any risk from any of the artists or their teams. They were all in the same boat. In show business, people see lights and glamour. They don't see that in events like this, the artist is standing in the dark, in mud, next to the smelly Portaloos, waiting to go home.

Some big artists that I have met have been really down to earth. Frank Sinatra was probably the biggest star in the world when we toured with him in 1975. On that tour of European capitals, he had security for sure. He needed it! But backstage it wasn't swarming with burly men stopping everyone at every turn.

As we left the gate to go to my car, I was papped by photographers waiting outside the gate. There were quite a few Nolans' fans waiting too who wanted a photo with me and an autograph. They said nice things about my set and how sad they were that I hadn't been on the tour. I have such happy memoires of the Pride event that year. Gay people have always followed the Nolans and our solo careers and we have always been grateful for their support. Throughout the 1990s and 2000s we appeared at just about every major gay nightclub in the UK. I can honestly say that they are some of the best audiences we have ever had. They watch and listen to you and cheer at the right places. They always come and see you after the show to say how good they thought you were. None of our family has ever had an issue with gay people and so it was an honour to have appeared at what is now believed to be the second largest pride event in the world.

It was now nearly time for the birth of my first grandchild. I went to Manchester with Amy and Vinny's paternal grandmother. Jean, Alex and Steve were already there. At the stated time for the birth, we were in a side room and we could see most of what was going on through a window. Everything seemed to be going fine and after a little while my first grandchild was born. We were all very excited and Steve even gave us the thumbs-up. All of a sudden though, things changed. I noticed the doctor seemed to be doing CPR on Vinny. We were terrified but after a minute or so we were told he was OK but that we could only have a quick glimpse of him as he needed to go to ICU as soon as possible.

It was such an anxious time. Normally the surgeon would put the bowel back into the abdomen and close the defect but because the abdominal cavity was small, and Vinny was not quite as well as he should have been a sort of mesh sack was stitched around it and it was manipulated back into the abdomen bit by bit every day until there was only a little bit left outside and then he would have an operation to insert the remainder. The operation would have to be done under general anaesthetic which is traumatic for a baby less than a month old.

It was a very hard time for Alex and Steve, seeing their little boy in an incubator and not being able to touch him. That went on for almost a month. Steve was working in Blackpool and commuted every day to the hospital in Manchester to see Alex and his new baby boy. Alex had to express her milk and even then, she couldn't actually give it to her baby because it had to be fed to him through a tube. As much as she was terribly upset about her baby suffering, I was also upset about watching my baby Alex suffer. It really was a terrible time for all of us.

After about a month Vinny had the operation and he came through wonderfully well. He was certainly a little fighter. He came out of surgery after a few hours and began to recover in no time at all.

Everybody was fantastic. We received cards, flowers and gifts by the bucketful. People were so kind; even members of the public got in touch. Our fans rose to the occasion. They always do. Those fans who had followed us around the country had watched Amy and Alex grow up. My girls knew most of the fans by name and had become used to getting lots of cards for their birthdays from people who they hardly knew. My brothers and sisters all got in touch to say how excited they were about becoming great aunts and uncles.

I fell in love with Vinny the second I saw his first scan picture. I had carried it with me and thrust it in the face of anyone who showed the slightest bit of interest. I adore all babies, if I see one in a restaurant, I usually stop what I am doing and go over to chat with the mother and coo over the baby. Heaven knows what these people must think when they see me zooming in on their child with a big smile on my face. Vinny was to be no exception. When I saw him for the first time my heart exploded with love. He had, and still has, these enormous blue eyes. He looked so fragile in the incubator with tubes and wires coming out of his little body. I wanted to pick him up and hold him forever, but of course you can't.

The birth of Vinny had given me the biggest boost. Although I was upset over the rift within our family, I was able to enjoy the last part of 2009.

As if it wasn't depressing enough not to be part of the tour, I then had a call from a documentary company who were making an hour-length film about the girls' career. Would I have any photographs of the act from early on our career? Would I mind if they would use photographs that included me in the programme? – WHAT!

They wanted to use my image and talk about me in a documentary when I was available to speak and answer for myself?

If this documentary was going to be about how the Nolans found success, then they should need to include me. But I wasn't having any of this rubbish. I was not going to be wiped out of the act and then take part in a documentary about how great we were and talk about all the great and awful times we had endured along the way only to finish and say that I am not included in this whole project but that it is great; oh, and I wish them all well with their tour!

They were going to feature my brothers who, let's face it, had nothing to lose, they had only been in the original line-up 'The Singing Nolans' in the early seventies. They had gone on to have careers outside of show business, so for them it was great. The people who make these programmes aren't interested in anything other than telling a story. If I had gone on and said how I felt, how would I know it would have been included anyway?

It was that kind of insensitivity that I found hurtful. Denise never expected to be part of this tour and album. She had left the act before the hits came. This show, however, glossed over her real contribution to our success. She was beyond heartbroken to find the family in this state. There is no one more family orientated than Denise and I could see how badly it had affected her. We noticed that when she talked about what was happening, her head started to shake. We were worried that she had developed Parkinson's disease, but it wasn't. Doctors believed it was stress that had brought it on.

My decision not to take part in the documentary was mine alone. So I can't complain that I was never given the chance to say what I wanted on camera, but I stand by the decision. It had to be better than me being shown in pictures or talking to camera as if I was endorsing what they were doing. It was a dreadful situation with me torn between anger, embarrassment, hurt and sadness.

When things happened with my sisters, I usually hear it third hand. Amy and Alex had stayed in touch with their aunties, which I encouraged. It still hurt like mad when they would say they were off to Coleen's for the night or going to one of the other's houses for a party but I never complained aloud.

When it came to the tour itself, I really didn't want to know about it. It was too painful. One of the dates was in Blackpool, at the Opera House. Some work colleagues had bought tickets as soon as it was announced. When they realised what had happened, they sold them on eBay which brought me some cheer.

I wasn't stupid enough to think that people would stay away en-masse. I am sure they would have been happy for me to be on stage with the girls, but I was realistic enough to know that the majority would also be happy to see any of The Nolans on stage. I had heard that backing singers had been used and loads of backing dancers. They had make-up artists, hairdressers and catering. I wanted to be there. I should have been there. There was no commercial or musical reason for me not being on stage with them. My ability merited me being on stage as well and it would have been fantastic to have been on the tour bus, having a laugh with them, just like the old times. When the reality of it sank in, I felt sick to the stomach. Made worse by the fact that they were in every newspaper I looked in. It was not a pleasant month, and I was glad when it was all over. They released a DVD, so there was a little more TV promotion. Fortunately, I was able to avoid reading and seeing the majority of it. The DVD sold quite well, but I couldn't bring myself to watch it. I still haven't.

At Christmas we had arranged to have the Christmas meal at Denise and Tom's. Denise had purchased a new dining table for their home, which eventually arrived two days before Christmas. Denise and Tom like to make provision and this table was huge! We would have to throw the salt and pepper to each other.

We were able to have a normal Christmas with the small gang that we had now got used to being around. Tom would be demonstrating his culinary skills that year. Tom is a gigantic personality. He is extravagant with his generosity and with his gestures. He had purchased the most enormous turkey I have ever seen. It was like the ones you see in American films. I'm sure it would have fed the entire street. He had gone out and purchased giant bain-marie warmers and prawns so big that they were a meal in their own right. We love a prawn cocktail on Christmas Day. You can take the girls out of the seventies, but you cannot take the seventies out of the girls. We did get visitors as the night wore on, including my brother Tommy and his kids, Tommy and Laura.

New Year was very quiet. In fact, that is just how we liked it. I was glad to see the back of 2009, to be honest.

2010 started with Bernie appearing on the ITV show *Popstars To Opera Stars.* Bernie was sensational on the show. Both Bernie and I have soprano voices although the tones in our voices are different. I knew how powerful Bernie's vocals really were and there was no better platform to demonstrate them than on this show. She sailed through each round. I think she would have won with my votes alone and she deserved to win. It turned out that, at the Grand Final, Bernie had lost by 0.5%. She was crowned runner-up having come top of the leader board in every episode of the series. It was felt that she had chosen the wrong song to sing in the final. There was also some dispute over who was going to sing which song with Rolando Villazón and Katherine Jenkins. In my opinion Bernie was by far the better opera singer and there has never been any doubt that Bernie had a phenomenal voice.

Chapter 4

Not Again

2010

In May I was folding my clothes fresh out of the dryer when my phone began to vibrate on my bedside locker. As I answered, I heard a very familiar voice on the end of the line; it was Maureen. I didn't know it was her because I had changed my number and didn't have her saved as a contact as we were still not on speaking terms.

I heard a shaky voice say, "Hi Anne, it's Maureen."

I immediately could tell there was something wrong. She was so upset as she told me that Bernie had been diagnosed with breast cancer. I sat down on the edge of my bed for a few moments and let the news sink in. I was devastated. I went in and out of listening to Maureen on the phone as I had dozens of questions running through my head. She told me that Bernie noticed there had been a change in the shape of her breast and soon after some dimpling in the breast tissue.

She went to visit her GP who had been able to feel a lump. Further tests confirmed that there were three lumps in her breast and significant calcification, which was a sure sign. She had a mammogram and a biopsy carried out the same day. They would let her know later on what the results were, but said they knew she had cancer.

The doctors discussed with Bernie the options and they decided the best course of action was to remove her breast and begin a course of chemotherapy immediately. They would also do a reconstruction at the same time. Not all cancers are the same. In my case I had the lump removed and then chemo and radiation. Linda had the operation, then the chemo and then reconstruction.

Bernie was to start the chemotherapy before the operation and had called some of the family to tell them and asked the others to let the rest of us know. I immediately called Bernie and said that if there was anything I could do she only had to ask. Even if it was to just chat. I told her I could take time off work to help out with Erin if needed. We may have been in the middle of an argument, but Bernie was still my sister and I loved her.

That was something that no one could ever take away. I love all of my sisters. Bernie thanked me, reassuring me that everything was under control and that she had *'Got this'*. For my part I felt numb with sadness. My instinct was to offer support and love. I also knew that a lot of things had been said, on both sides. It would be very difficult for any of us to just wipe the slate clean after all that had happened.

This row! It just wouldn't go away. There had been lots of instances where it had a knock-on effect. Besides the obvious impact on our immediate family, we had lots of friends who were mutual to all of us. We often had the same friends and would consider lots of them as family.

When friends were having christenings or weddings, they would feel awkward and not want to invite both camps, as they saw it. They often chose the group with the most people in it. It almost felt like being one half of a divorced couple. One or both divorcees were left out in the cold because people simply didn't know who to invite.

As I've said before, there were things said on both sides. I got together with Denise to write an open letter to the girls to see if we could accept what had happened and move forward. We outlined what we saw as a very real problem and added, "For the sake of our family and the wider circle of mutual friends, we should be civil to one another."

I don't think the letter had hit the doormat at Maureen's house before she called to say that she wanted to find a way forward, for us to be friends again. Bernie was also quick to reply. However, it would have needed a little bit more time and healing for the relationships with Coleen and Linda to heal themselves.

Now I was in regular contact with Bernie I was able to offer her support and friendship. Although Bernie and I had a pretty fiery relationship in the past when growing up, I was always her biggest fan as a singer. She had such power in her voice. She was only 5' 1" in height and people were always surprised that such a huge voice could come out of such a tiny person. She was very determined and strong. If anyone was up for the fight against cancer it was Bernie.

They had recently moved to Weybridge, so it was difficult for all the family to visit Weybridge as we all lived up north. We did speak on the phone a lot. Maureen was away working on the musical *Blood Brothers* and I also tried to call her as well.

After her run in *Blood Brothers*, Maureen flew out to Spain to get married. She had been with Richie for years. They had lived together for twenty-odd years before they decided to get hitched.

She had asked most of her sisters to be bridesmaids and that hurt. The three eldest sisters, Denise, Maureen and I had always been so close. The girls had a new management company which they all signed to and which looked after all of their work. They had organised a big magazine to cover the whole wedding day and have Bernie, Linda, Coleen and Maureen's son Danny's girlfriend Maddison be her bridesmaids.

This was particularly sad as we had always had all the sisters as bridesmaids at each other's weddings.

Word came back to me that Maureen was also really upset that she couldn't find a way for us to share her special day. As we were speaking to both her and Bernie by now, I can only assume that the wedding had been organised for Maureen beforehand, as we had only been talking for a couple of months.

Even though we were on speaking terms we weren't at the stage yet to jet off altogether for a holiday and watch Maureen walk down the aisle. This is one of the saddest things following the aftermath of the tour. It had spoiled the chance for us to be together for such a joyful day. Aunty was really upset.

When a magazine covers a wedding, none of the guests are allowed to take pictures of their own. I had to wait until the magazine came out before I could see what she looked like on her special day. She looked beautiful; she always does. It was the first time that I had seen Bernie wearing her wig. She had a real hair one made in the style she most recently wore. They all looked so happy in the photographs.

It had been touch and go whether Bernie would be able to attend at all. She was coming to the end of her cancer treatment and had been really ill. She had chemotherapy drugs inside her and had suffered with mouth ulcers, sore feet and all the sickness that came with the treatment. The medics were optimistic that they had caught her cancer in time and that was something positive to hold on to.

Chapter 5

The Beverley Hillbillies

2011

A couple of months after the wedding, Denise and Tom decided to have a big USA holiday. Denise's partner, Tom has a son who lives in Los Angeles. He goes there most years to see him. Myself, Amy, Alex & Steve, and their gorgeous baby Vinny, who was just coming up to his first birthday, along with Aunty and my brother's daughter Laura, decided to join them. I detest flying, so a thirteen-hour flight to Los Angeles did not fill me with great joy. We were lucky though. We got good seats with Virgin and any fears we might have had about Vinny causing any disruptions on the flight, as toddlers often do, quickly vanished. When we arrived Stateside, we were like hillbillies, we were knackered!

We had an incredible time, our first week and a half was spent in Los Angeles which was a fantastic thrill, as Hollywood films were a big part of our childhood. We went into Hollywood and drove around looking at all the beautiful houses belonging to some of our favourite Hollywood stars. We saw the Dolby theatre where the Oscars take place and the Hollywood Walk of Fame.

In the second week we drove to Las Vegas and stayed at the MGM Grand on the Vegas strip. When we arrived, I put a twenty-dollar bet on the first roulette table I came across at the hotel. I had heard it was traditional to do this even before you check in. I am not usually lucky, but I won four hundred dollars. We visited all the fantastic hotels and had dinner at the Venetian on Laura's birthday, which my winnings helped to pay for.

We did all the fabulous rides and experiences. One highlight was an early morning helicopter flight over the Grand Canyon, which was a truly exhilarating experience. Vinny was just over a year old so, although he wouldn't remember it later on, he had a ball.

With Vinny in Las Vegas

Back in LA we took Vinny to Disney where he met all his favourite characters. The sheer delight on his face when he came face to face with Mickey Mouse and Snow White is a memory that won't leave me. Vinny was a fabulous baby. We all called him 'Rent A Child' and the Americans referred to him as a 'Gerber Baby' which was apparently the face of a beautiful baby on an advert for baby food. He was so well behaved with whoever looked after him. Alex and Steve didn't like to be away from him for very long, but if they did have a night out or needed a babysitter then they were never short of volunteers.

With him being my first grandchild, I'd become somewhat possessive of him. I would offer to have him at any time. I was almost sixty years old myself and I must admit that sometimes after he went back to his mum and dad, I was exhausted. Still, I wouldn't swap a single minute of it.

Very early on in Vinny's life we could tell that he was a special child. He was extraordinarily alert and forward. We would often look at one another open mouthed when he had done something and say we had never seen a one-year-old do that. Of course, he wanted toys and teddies, but he had more of an interest in things like jigsaws and toys where he was using his mind.

In America he was in fine form. When we look at pictures of that holiday it is obvious he was in his element. We took a day trip from Los Angeles to Big Bear Mountain which Denise and Tom had visited on previous occasions. It was like something out of a Hollywood movie with log cabins and cute little shops. We decided that one day we would visit it again at Christmastime. We stayed in Los Angeles for the remainder of our holiday, visiting Tom's family in Rancho Cucamonga. We spent a wonderful day there at their beautiful home on the outskirts of LA. The rest of our holiday was spent swimming, sunbathing, and eating in lovely restaurants, truly a most wonderful holiday.

I would be turning sixty a few weeks after returning from America. I had reserved a room at a local venue for November 12th which was a Friday. Denise turned into a military grade party planner. She organised two bands, a DJ, food and cakes. I wanted everyone there who mattered to me. There was no doubt in my mind that I was going to invite all of my sisters. Bernie said she would come over even though she had not long since finished her cancer treatment.

She had recently made headlines when she attended a TV award show with her head shaved bald. Bernie was never blessed with a thick mane of hair and her aggressive treatment of the cancer had seen her pale blonde tresses fall out early on. She made the choice to shave the whole lot off. I must confess she really suited it. She had a gorgeous elf-like face and a lovely shaped head. Only a person as confident as Bernie could carry that off. It also brought the interest of the TV shows who wanted to interview her about it. It seems really superficial to chat about her bald head when it was as a result of chemotherapy, not a fashion statement but it did give her the chance to tell her story and raise awareness for people who were in the same position her.

Luckily for me though, Maureen was due to star in the West End Production of *Blood Brothers*, but not until November 22nd. She would be able to come to my party and that meant such a lot; I was really happy with the progress I was making with rebuilding my relationships with Bernie and Maureen. However, I knew there was work to do with Linda & Coleen, so I extended an olive branch and sent them both invitations to my party.

I am very close to a Blackpool family called the Hetheringtons. They are a huge family like we Nolans and they wanted to provide the catering for my party which was great. They ran a catering company and did it at a great rate for us. They made up a chilli, a hot pot, a curry as well as crusty bread, rice, salad and a cold buffet.

Years and years ago, when we were the Singing Nolans, Frank Flynn was our musical director. Now he worked with his wife in a local band. Their son, Andy, fronts his own band – Flip! I can't tell you just how good they are. On the face of it, it sounds strange. Andy sings lead vocals and plays two large tom-tom drums. Two other musicians, Alan and Heath, play guitar and fiddle. They cover songs from artists such as Lionel Richie and Stevie Wonder. You would think that such an odd combination of instruments would not be able to have such a big sound, but they really do. Andy is a great singer too. We had a swing band that was able to play so the rest of us could sing.

Denise sang a couple of songs including 'This Is My Life', made famous by Shirley Bassey, which Denise sang brilliantly. I sang 'Over The Rainbow' in the style of Eva Cassidy and also 'Footloose'. My brothers, Brian and Tommy, also did a spot. My best friend Jacqui had helped with a load of old photographs and pinned them up all around the room. Jacqui has always had my back. In fact, two more of my best friends also came. Patsy and Joan, we have been friends since I first came to England in 1962. We have all become aunties to our respective children and still see each other as often as we can. Jacqui, in particular, has been a tower of strength to me. She knows every one of my family and I can't ever imagine the four of us ever falling out. I don't think they have ever seen me as one of the Nolans. They see me as Anne Wilson and we know each other inside and out. We always laugh and enjoy each

With my best friends Joan, Patsy and Jacqui

other's company. There is almost a secret language that goes on between the four of us.

I also invited some of my show business friends, amongst whom were Bobby Ball, Johnnie Casson and Mia Carla. It was a magical evening. Vinny watched with eyes that made me think *this boy has show business in his blood.* His mum had even dressed him with a bow tie. Amy and Alex had ordered a huge cake with gold lettering and icing. The room was packed and I had the time of my life; everyone seemed to know everyone else and they all mingled together. Bernie turned up quite late looking gorgeous in a black dress and she looked radiant. She joined Flip! on stage and sang the Chaka Khan number 'Ain't Nobody'. It was as if she had never been ill at all. It might not be perfect, but I saw the green shoots of recovery on my family tree.

Bernie at my 60th

In December, I discovered that one of our albums, *20 Giant Hits*, was set to be re-released. There was not to be any royalties due though. Although that album had been released several times, we had never had a penny from it. There had been discussions a few times over the years with a view to giving us a share of its profits. This time the album had a complete remaster and a bonus CD of all our early singles that had again been remastered. These songs had not had a CD release before. In our early years we had signed up with managers who gave us a contract that offered us a salary. It transpired that as our success grew and therefore our fees, our salary stayed the same. We were not entitled to any cash from record sales either. The situation only improved when we joined CBS. One year the *X Factor* show used 'I'm In The Mood For Dancing' for almost every commercial break. We did get a substantial cheque for that which was a nice little boost, especially just before Christmas.

That year we once again went to Denise's for dinner. She was appearing in Bridlington and had to leave on Christmas Day after dinner. Amy had a chap in her life too. She had known him since she was fifteen and they seemed well suited at the start. She and I were living under the same roof at my Aunty Teresa's house who was just amazing with me.

Everyone knew that following my divorce and the loss of my home, I was, for want of a better word, on the bones of my backside. After I moved in with my aunt, she gave me free rein to do what I wanted in the house. She started by having an extension built with a bedroom and bathroom. Her legs were riddled with arthritis, so stairs had become a problem for her. She had her own sitting room and let me have the rest of the house. I had central heating installed, new double glazing with new flooring in the hall and my lounge. I don't think I had been as contented as I was for a very long time. My daughters had found happiness and I was settled into a great routine.

I had a mini residency at the Sands Venue in Blackpool in the early part of 2011. It was a gorgeous new night spot on the promenade. Unlike most night clubs this place was aimed at people over the age of thirty! There was a seven-piece swing band. All the tables were placed around the dance floor and it was so plush with no expense spared. The owners of the venue were part of the Wilkinson family who had established themselves as a major High Street retailer. They had opened a similar place in Leicester and wanted to stake a claim in Blackpool. This place had all the feel of a Las Vegas night spot. Denise and Tom had discovered it when it first opened. During the night Denise was in conversation with the bosses who seemed keen to book her. She had a few great shows there that were very well attended. Then they asked me to put together a set. I wouldn't be able to use the one I used at Manchester Pride as this venue was aimed at jazz and swing fans so I used music from the bands repertoire including 'Chicago' and 'Fly Me To The Moon' and one of my favourites, 'Don't Rain On

My Parade', the Barbra Streisand classic. Altogether I did the Sands three times and loved every appearance.

The Sands itself couldn't sustain such a high level of musicianship and standard of service without it being packed solid every night and I didn't know if Blackpool had the kind of visitors who would support it. Needless to say, the next year they began putting on shows that were more populist in their appeal. A tribute show was the main show the following year with Freddie Mercury, Elvis, and George Michael impersonators. The menu was also changed to accommodate that and the music which most of my family love was pushed aside. I can understand the business logic with this decision as the bottom line is profit. If an act can use a backing tape the cost of musicians is saved and audiences don't seem to mind. The facts are that quality shows cost money. I am not saying the new music was not high quality, just different.

We made enquiries into hiring the venue for our next big party, but it was too high. Instead, we secured the hire of a cabaret night club on Central Pier in Blackpool for Amy's 30th birthday. Where had all the time gone we wondered? Amy had by now taken a job outside show business, working alongside me at the Insolvency Service. She was seeing her chap most nights and they seemed happy.

For the party Amy had decided she wanted it to be fancy dress and it came as no real surprise what the theme was to be – Disney! All of us are Disney crazy. Amy had very distinct ideas about what she wanted. She was going to have a live band, a DJ and a sweet shop. Her friend Kelly came up with the shop, complete with little paper bags. The catering came once more via our friends, the Hetheringtons.

The costumes that people put together were hysterical. I had gone as the Queen of Hearts; Amy was Minnie Mouse, complete with those massive shoes Minnie wears! Alex was Jessica Rabbitt. Denise made a fine attempt at Maid Marion and Maureen came straight after her show, arriving just before midnight in the guise of Mary Poppins. Everyone must have spent a small fortune on their outfits. I had also made a video similar to the one I had done for Alex.

The venue really let me down though. They had insisted they had a screen we could use and the laptop holding the file could be wired into their sound system. On the night they wouldn't allow us to plug the laptop in. As a backup we had the video on a DVD that they let us use in a player behind the bar. The sound was awful as the screen was at one side of the room and the speakers at the other. There was a second or two's time lag and we could barely hear the song; *'Amy'* that had been written especially for her by Robin Smith our musical director when we first started touring. He was also Coleen's first love and the song was recorded on the Nolan's album dedicated to Amy when she was born. Despite the sound quality, I don't think it detracted from the overall evening's enjoyment too much.

Sadly, on that night Amy had an argument with her chap and they ended up splitting up. Amy had been in a bad relationship before, and I didn't like the idea of her going down that road again. She had been arguing with him quite a lot and it came as no surprise that they split. Because I am so close to my girls there is a line that I cross. I am also their friend as well as their mother. Like all friends I have an opinion over what's the best thing to do but always accept the final decision is for the girls to make. Although Amy was six years older than Alex, she was more of a free spirit. She had her own style in clothes and is a kind and trusting soul. In lots of ways I am glad that some of the knocks that life have thrown at us all have not hardened Amy.

Bernie hadn't been able to make it to Amy's party. She had just agreed to take part in the UK tour of *Calendar Girls*. This was a remarkable achievement. Not only had she seemingly made a full recovery, but she was to tastefully go topless for the show, which was about the Yorkshire Women's Institute members who had almost bared all to raise money for charity. Bernie had undergone reconstructive surgery and for many women the show would have been a challenge to say the least but Bernie relished the chance to appear in the musical production.

Naturally, I wasn't altogether pleased when it emerged that my sisters had decided to write another book. It was scheduled to be released in April. I didn't mind them writing about any of our group's achievements or about their own personal lives. What I was bothered about was that the scars of our recent troubles hadn't fully healed. I vowed not to read it and told all my friends that they shouldn't tell me any of its contents. Fortunately, they all respected my wishes.

Later on, I found that they were going to write separate chapters as individuals that would chart how each person would feel about a particular event. If anything, it opened some old wounds that had long been buried between them. The book was a commercial success of course and they appeared on lots of chat shows.

In late summer, Amy shocked us all by announcing she was pregnant. She instantly decided she was going to keep the baby. Very early in the pregnancy Amy began to show, unlike Alex, who was barely a dress size bigger until the seventh or eighth month.

Bernie turned fifty in October. I waited to see how this would play out and was delighted when she invited us all to her party in London. She even asked if I wanted to sing, the evening was spectacular. Her musical director made sure that all our song choices were in the right key to suit our voices. She employed a band and invited some of her show business friends including Peter Cox with whom she had recorded a duet on her debut album which had been released a short time before. He brought the place to its feet with a rousing version of 'Your Sex Is On Fire'. My family from Dublin including Valerie, Sharron, Lorraine and Angie came over for the party. We have always been very close to the girls who are my mum's brother, Charlie's, daughters. We danced the night away and celebrated our beautiful Bernie.

In the vast function room the tables were dressed with white linen cloths and beautiful table arrangements. There was so much attention to detail for the big night. Linda and Coleen were there and we smiled at each other but sat at different tables. There was no anger or comments exchanged as we are all adults and enjoyed celebrating our beautiful sister's birthday after the traumatic year she had been through.

Chapter 6

Just One Voice

2012

Shortly after I got home from Bernie's party in London I got a call from my manager.

"You're going to make an album."

My first reaction was to laugh. Then I said to him "Oh, just like that?"

He went on to tell me that he would be coming back to the UK to live for a while and that he had made contact with a record producer who had a studio in Weston-Super-Mare.

In February I made the trip there for a long weekend. I met the guy from the studio called Brian Monk who was a lovely man. We tossed ideas around and one of them was to go right back to my Irish roots and have an album of Irish lullabies and traditional folk songs. It is a unique market which has its fans and I was certainly up for exploring the genre. Another option was to have a dance album. This was the one that I was least attracted to. Cilla Black had recently worked with the Almighty label. They take songs and either rework them in their original format or get the artist to re-record the tracks and then give them a heavy dance remix. Some of my other friends thought this was a great idea, but not me. The format we went for in the end was a covers album.

I have some regrets about how the album came together. I was carried along by a lot of things. Some of the tracks that were selected would not have jumped out at me had I been choosing them entirely by myself. I always sang the highest notes when performing as one of the Nolans but the producers of the album wanted to use my lower register and my softer voice. It made recording quite taxing, having to record the songs several times until they found the keys they wanted.

We released a single prior to releasing the album to test the water and lots of radio stations wanted me to appear on their shows. I travelled to BBC Blackburn on one day where they could link me up to all the other BBC radio stations in the country. I must have done about fifteen in one day. Every time before the interview started, I would get about a minute to talk about the new single and that I had donated some of the royalties to the Save The Children appeal for babies in Bangladesh.

However, before long, in almost every interview, the disc jockey would direct the chat towards my sisters and the argument. They wanted to talk about their tour again and it was so frustrating. After lots of plugging away by my manager at the time, Marc, I was finally given a spot as a guest on the *Gabby Logan Show* on Channel 5.

It was to be the first time I would appear on TV as a solo artist and sing live. I cannot begin to tell you how nervous I was in the green room. Also on the show was Paul Nicholas who had made a name for himself in musical theatre. He had, in recent years become an impresario in his own right, with major shows in the West End.

Gabby was lovely. She gave me a lovely warm-up introduction before inviting me to have a chat with her. We skirted over the family row and talked about the tour we had been on as the support act to Frank Sinatra. It all went well. I then had to sing live.

I know I had been singing as a solo artist for many years. Even when I was in the Nolans, I had starred in panto on my own, but I had never done a song alone on TV. The studio was small with only a small audience present but I knew that millions would be at home watching which is so nerve racking. The show had been kind enough to allow me to sing anything I wanted. Some of the tracks that I had recorded for the album had been finished so I picked 'If I Could' which I always loved. It was a cover of the Barbra Streisand song that I had played at Alex's 21st. I think I pulled it off, although I only sang a verse and afterwards everyone was really complimentary about my performance.

A couple of weeks later, we were at home when several of Amy's friends came to my house and inevitably the topic of baby names came up. It seems people have stopped calling their kids Peter, Mark and

Paul. Amy ran a few names by us. She suggested Ryder, Rourke and Devon. To my mind they weren't even names. What did I know though?

Amy had been planning her baby's delivery with military precision. Right on cue she went into labour the day before Denise was having her 60th birthday party. Amy had split from her boyfriend for good now and it hadn't got to the stage yet where they were able to speak properly. Nevertheless, to her credit she had organised everything herself.

She had bought the vast majority of things that she needed. I had helped as much as Amy would allow. Her aunties all wanted to be in on the action too. She attended all the scans and antenatal classes. It's not easy for a woman who is alone to be pregnant. Not that there is any stigma anymore, it is just the sheer hard work of the whole thing. There are always appointments to keep and places to go. As well as all the shopping, her friend, Laura Higgins, one of the Hetherington family, had hit on the idea of a 'baby shower', which was held at Denise's house. She has some wonderful friends and they all turned up with sack loads of gifts such as Moses baskets and car seats. She had enough romper suits and baby grows to open a shop of her own. Other people gave gifts like talcum powder, Sudocrem and even nappies. All the gifts were handy and all would get used. Laura had devised party games that were great fun, although guessing which flavour baby food was smeared on a nappy didn't do a lot for my stomach!

The baby 'shower thing' was fairly new in the UK as far as I am aware. It's one of the things from America that I really approve of, that and trick or treat at Halloween.

Amy had decided she would have three people as her birth partners. She had chosen the water delivery suite at Blackpool's Victoria Hospital. They only had two such rooms so had to be booked well in advance, so the mother had to hope baby came along at the right time. She chose to have Alex and me together with Laura Higgins. Laura had two children of her own and was very clued up. She is also a very solid individual who is not fazed by anything. If anything were to go wrong, I can't think of anyone more capable than Laura to have in your corner. It was really exciting, but at the same time very tranquil in the room with the birthing pool. Amy had a great big bag with her. It contained every kind of snack that you can imagine. She had soft drinks CDs and, believe me, when I tell you this; she also had a card game – Uno.

We all love that game and have spent many an hour laughing while we play it. I didn't have the heart to tell Amy that once she was in the throes of labour, she wouldn't be up for playing any kind of card game. I think she was lulled into a false sense of security because the pregnancy itself had gone without a hitch. I didn't have a clue what she thought the birth was going to be like, but I just couldn't let her know that what was soon coming up was not going to be like a Saturday night slumber party with her mates.

She was perfectly calm at the start and played CDs of her favourite music quietly in the background. The nurses and her midwife were coming in regularly to keep checking her and were happy with the progress.

As the night went on nothing seemed to be happening that would indicate a baby was due any time soon and Amy had by now settled herself in the birthing pool and was still very calm. I thought it was all really pleasant to be fair. The idea of sitting in the pool wouldn't have appealed to me, but it wasn't me that was having the baby!

Just then a midwife came in and checked Amy. The normal time to start pushing was when the neck of the cervix dilates to 10cm. The midwife was chirpy and said, "OK Amy, you can start to push now if you feel the need to."

She was having regular contractions and as any mother will tell you, you want to push as soon as they start. You are taught throughout the pregnancy at antenatal classes about this sort of thing. With the midwife giving her approval, Amy pushed and at the next contraction, she pushed again. Nothing was happening except that Amy was now in considerable pain. Each push brought even more pain and before long she was in agony. She had now had enough of the wretched birthing pool and wanted out, so the staff placed her on a bed. When another midwife checked Amy's cervix she declared that it was nowhere near the 10cm that was required and that she should not have been pushing at all. The next thing that happened sent us all into a blind panic. Amy haemorrhaged. It was terrifying. All at once a whole army of doctors and nurses came flooding in the room. There was blood everywhere. With very little effort from Amy the baby was born. It was as if he had just fallen out. Amy was in excruciating pain. One of the doctors seemed to throw the baby in my arms, wrapped in a robe and said, "Here you take him, and stand over there; don't get in the way."

Everything was happening so quickly. My own first baby had been a massive trauma and here I was witnessing my first daughter go through what looked like carnage. At one point I noticed that one of the doctors had her entire fist inside Amy, stemming the bleeding. They carried out what they needed to do and perhaps it only took a matter of minutes but for the three of us in that room with no medical training, it seemed to have taken hours. After a short time, the baby was cleaned up, as was Amy. She was very emotional and no doubt, sore as she had to have multiple sutures. Thankfully the room was soon cleared of blood and Amy rested, but not for long. Like every mother she instantly fell in love with him and wanted to be next to him, holding him and loving him.

She turned to me, with tears in her eyes and said, "Mum, I've been looking for the man of my dreams, and now I think I've found him."

Ryder Devon Rourke was born on Thursday 5th April at 8.32 a.m. Mother and baby were fine, but the grandmother was absolutely knackered.

Meanwhile Tom, Denise's chap, had decided to hire the Sands Venue for Denise's 60th birthday. By the time the party date arrived, I think Denise was heading for a nervous breakdown. She wanted everything to be perfect. Tom decided to get a banner printed. He had a lovely picture of Denise put on it together with an English and Irish flag entwined. He made the mistake of allowing the printers to insert the traditional Irish greeting of *Céad Míle Fáilte* which roughly translates as 'A Hundred Thousand Welcomes'. The printers had assured him they knew how to write it but when it was unveiled on the day of the party it read *"Caed Mele Failite"*. Denise was furious but it was masked by the clever use of balloons. A lot of Denise's friends from London and people she had met during her many showbiz years made the journey from various parts of the country all the way to Blackpool. Shane and Jake also came to Denise's party, and I think that made her night.

Everyone wore their finest outfits. Tom and Denise had paid for a magnificent meal and the seven-piece orchestra. Some of our friends sang, as did everyone in the family. Everyone recorded a birthday greeting for her and she was made to feel the belle of the ball. She and I had rehearsed a great surprise number to sing together. We were going to sing the Judy Garland and Barbra Streisand duet 'Happy Days/Get Happy'. That might sound easy when you read it but, in fact, they are two completely different songs. Both well known in their own right.

You can see the original live version on YouTube. The song is sung in what is called counter-melody. The musical accompaniment was provided by a fantastic pianist called Dave Bintley, who was also a good friend. He plays a melody and Denise was due to start with 'Forget your troubles come on get happy'. As she sings the word 'troubles' I begin to sing, "Happy days are here again the skies above are clear…" Both songs have been changed slightly to work with each other. About a minute into the song, I looked at Denise and said, "I really have no idea what is going on but this is not how I remember rehearsing it."

Denise said into the microphone, "Anne has had a bit too much to drink and can't remember the song."

I agreed, as I really couldn't work out what was wrong. We were both in hysterics, and then all of a sudden Denise again said into the microphone, "Oh my God it's not Anne that's been doing it wrong, it's me! I have been singing Anne's part instead of mine, obviously *I'm* the one who's had too much to drink." Well at least it explained why we were making such a cock up of it all.

On the fourth attempt we sang it right and, afterwards, people came up to tell us how great it was. Very soon I wasn't really up for singing much more. I had toasted the birthday girl one too many times. I am not much of a drinker and it doesn't take much for a drink to go to my head. That night turned out to be another fabulous evening. When our family and friends are all together there is always a great time to be had.

Chapter 7

'All You Need Is Love'

Throughout 2012 Bernie was appearing as Mama Morton in the UK touring production of *Chicago*. This was to be one of Bernie's most iconic roles. There was something about hearing her voice soar across massive theatres. When she finished her big number, 'When You're Good To Mama', at almost every performance the audience would jump from their seats and give her a standing ovation.

The production would typically stay a week in each town, and usually she would have every Sunday off and, like the rest of us, she would travel all the way home for just one day with her family. Bernie had been going about her normal life, but on one such occasion, as she was at home getting ready to go for a meal with Steve when she felt a lump in her breast.

She chose to err on the side of caution and went to see the team at the hospital in Surrey where she had been treated before. They noticed the lump before she was even scanned and carried out a mammogram there and then and were not happy with what they found. She was told that she would need a biopsy, which they also did immediately. She went home and began preparing to go back into *Chicago* in Eastbourne on the Monday.

As it was the school holiday, she took Steve and Erin with her for a break, having performed all week. She had a phone call on the Friday telling her that her cancer had come back. She made her way home and doctors told her they felt it safe enough to remove the lump and have a course of radio therapy. At that time, only Steve and Bernie knew about the diagnosis. She had told some of the family she was having annual tests carried out and was looking forward to flying out to Monte Carlo where the show had been booked to play for a week.

Linda was staying at her house to look after Erin while Bernie was away and she had taken Linda into her confidence. Secretly she had a bone scan, a breast scan and a PET-CT scan carried out before she went to Monte Carlo. Considering how she shouldered all of that with just her and Steve, it makes you realise just how much of a fighter and a stage trooper she really was. The two of them went out to Monte Carlo leaving Erin with Linda. It should have been a lovely romantic city to visit, which I'm sure it was, but the trip must have been so tainted with what she was dealing with.

After returning home on the Sunday, she was gearing up for her operation, which had been scheduled to take place on the Tuesday. Her specialist called her on the Sunday night to ask her to go to the hospital the next morning. She protested, saying that she was due to have an operation on the Tuesday, but he stopped her in her tracks and said that she wasn't having any operation on Tuesday. He told her that her cancer had spread but wouldn't tell her on the phone where it had spread to. The next twelve hours must have been torture for them all. What she had to suffer that night was nothing to what hit her the next day at the hospital. Her specialist confirmed that the cancer had spread to her brain, her liver, her bones, and for a singer, perhaps the cruellest place of all, to her lungs.

The doctors told her that this time the cancer, which only a year earlier was deemed to have gone completely, had hidden and had now presented itself in all these places and spread like wildfire. This process is known as metastasis. He then delivered the knockout blow: this time her cancer was incurable. He added words of cold comfort saying that it was 'treatable, but not curable'. Bernie asked him the same question I suspect every person given that news asks, "How long have I got?" He told her they were talking 'years, but not many years.'

How anyone can compose themselves after being given that news is a mystery to me. I can only speak from my own cancer experience. You just do. What choice have you got? You can't fling yourself on the floor and demand they make you better and that you are not leaving until they do. I am sure they are used to people taking as long as they want to process the information and to people taking the news in lots of different ways.

I wanted to have more information and be with my family who were subconsciously calling me. Perhaps some patients get angry and, from what I was told, Bernie was all of those things. She shouted and got angry; she cried and felt depressed and went into denial, thinking that it wasn't happening to her. But that's the thing with this thing called cancer isn't it? It doesn't care if you are royalty, a cleaner or a pop singer.

Bernie called Maureen and Coleen on the phone and was rightly getting depressed with repeating the story and asked them to pass it on to the rest of us. Maureen called me and I could hardly understand what she was saying down the phone through her sobs. Eventually, the penny dropped and it sank in. I had the unenviable task of telling Aunty Teresa and the girls. Bernie had insisted she didn't want anyone else to know, which, in itself was difficult. People, like my friend Jacqui, had known Bernie since she was two years old. She had been like a sister to her and they adored each other. Amy and Alex were heartbroken, truly inconsolable. When they were old enough, and possibly for a while before that, Bernie had taken them on nights out. They had enjoyed countless boozy nights out, dancing at clubs and coming home at all hours. Not only was Bernie an aunty to them but she was also a friend. She had been someone they looked up to because of her immense talent and success. She was wise with her knowledge and advice without ever being preachy. She had used her connections in show businesses to get them into places and meet some of their heroes.

Shortly after, we were told that Bernie was going on a course of drugs and was also going to take part in some medical trial for a new wonder drug. She had been advised by people at the hospital that new drugs were coming on the market all the time. Cancer, they said, was not the death sentence that it used to be. They gave her the courage, self-determination and strength to give this her best shot. Bernie told me in conversation one night a while later that she couldn't wait to get on the drugs to 'Get this thing out of me'. She said that people at the hospital who had a similar kind of metastasis had lived for fifteen or twenty years. That seemed an incredible piece of news and I decided to run with that in my brain. Bernie had been given news which was the worst-case scenario, but that was not how it was going to pan out in reality.

Bernie didn't have to undergo the invasive intravenous chemotherapy this time. Instead, she was to have the anti-cancer drug Herceptin and chemo tablets. There was a chance that she was going to lose her hair again, but in the early stages it hung on in there. She then decided to tell Erin which must have been an incredible shock for her. Erin is a very mature girl and always had been, even when she was just thirteen. She took it very well, or as well as anyone can take hearing their mother had incurable cancer.

After a few weeks of treatment Bernie was told – miraculously – that the cancer in her brain had gone. She heard that the cancer in her lungs had been massively reduced too. She called to tell us all the great news. Whereas they knew they hadn't somehow cured Bernie, the treatment was working.

I went to see Bernie in *Chicago* in Liverpool with a couple of friends. It was the first time I had seen her in ages as her workload had been so heavy.

When I saw her at Christmas, her hair had grown back from her previous bout of chemotherapy, but it was grey and curly. Luckily, I hadn't lost all of mine the first time I had cancer, I just had it cut really short and bought a wig. I didn't really need the wig and it was hot and uncomfortable anyway. Amy used it a couple of years later when we did panto and she played Snow White!

I had seen Bernie a few times on TV and could see behind her eyes that she was suffering, but no one except her close family would have noticed that.

Bernie had to wait a while before she could have her hair coloured, so, by the time I saw her in Liverpool, it had grown to shoulder length. She had recently had it tinted and it was a lovely blonde colour, similar to how she had worn it for years. This reassured me, for she looked back to normal. She looked like the Bernie we all knew again which was comforting.

For the part of Mama Morton she had to wear her hair up in a plait and, before the show, we popped back to her dressing room where she spoke freely about how the show was going and said to us:

"Don't blink during this show or you will miss me." and we all laughed. She spoke a few whispered words which, although not in code, were not meant for all ears.

"Yeah, I'm at the hospital on Friday – but we don't need to talk about that."

It was her complete aura of calm that is strange to look back on now. Here was a successful woman, on the top of her game, doing what she loved to do. All the cast and crew loved her and she showed no nerves as she prepared to go on stage in front of thousands of people. I am not alone when I feel utter bewilderment as to why such a dreadful disease can so cruelly cut down a person in this way.

You have to carry on otherwise you would end up in a psychiatric ward. I guess it's part of our human DNA that gives us the ability to do just that. Linda joked at the time about her treatment and the way people were forever calling her 'brave'. The truth is, we are no braver than anyone else. You could refuse treatment and die quickly, or you can accept treatment. There is no third way, other than suicide and that is not a realistic option. I suppose the way a person handles things makes them brave or not. Bernie handled everything she had to go through wonderfully well so, as far as we were concerned, she was certainly brave.

Bernie told us to meet her after the show at the stage door. We went into the theatre and took our seats for the performance, and what a performance Bernie gave that night. Mind you she always did give her all in every performance.

Bernie appeared mainly in the first half of the show and sang only one solo song, but the quality that she brought to the part really stood out. Her vocals were as good, if not better, than I had ever heard and the dancing was outstanding with all Bob Fossey's choreography.

Bernie met us as arranged after the show, then, as she was about to get in her car to go home, we had a cuddle. There was real love and warmth in that embrace, which I think we both felt. It is a connection that perhaps only sisters can feel. Certainly it is a connection that says, no matter how big the argument and no matter how many words are said in anger, family will come through the other side.

I thought we really ought to see if there was a way to get that connection back with Coleen and Linda. But, as always in life, I had another challenge to face. This time, I would have my mettle tested to the very maximum over the next few weeks.

Alex and Steve had decided to get married. They had been together a few years now and their family were happy. I guess it's the natural thing to do. I hadn't put them under any pressure to get married but once the decision had been made, I was determined to make it the best wedding possible. I took the traditional responsibilities of mother of the bride seriously.

The bride's parents usually pay for the reception, the bride's and bridesmaids' dresses, stationery, the flowers and church. The groom is normally responsible for the cars, the honeymoon, his and the best man's and ushers' suits and gifts for the bridesmaids. My ex-husband, Brian, wasn't in a position financially to help me with the cost of the wedding, so Alex and Steve paid for the reception and everything the groom is responsible for and Steve's parents paid for the cars.

Alex and I traipsed around Blackpool and the surrounding areas to find a venue for the wedding and finally settled on The Grand Hotel on St Anne's promenade for both the wedding lunch and evening reception. We also thought about all the lovely churches in the area including our own parish but, in the end, they decided that they wanted to get married in a gorgeous church in St Anne's called Saint Joseph's. It is an older Catholic Church set in its own grounds and it was also close to the wedding hotel. My cousin, who is a Canon in the Catholic Church, would perform the ceremony after we got permission from the Parish Priest of St Josephs.

Churches can sometimes be a bit fussy when it comes to the use of their venues. We have had occasions where we have wanted to sing at a wedding and the priests have been insistent that there be no singing. Others have allowed it, as long as it was a religious song and not a pop song. Don't get me wrong, I am a regular at church and I love some of the beautiful hymns that we sing, but, equally, there are some truly poignant and inspiring popular songs that could have a spiritual meaning as well as a sentimental one.

This parish priest was happy to have Alex and Steve walk down the aisle to the tune 'The Prayer' sung by Charlotte Church and Josh Groban. It sounds simply stunning in church and made me go cold with emotion. I had arranged to have the church bells ringing as she entered and left the church. Vinny was going to carry the rings and she was to be assisted by no less than five bridesmaids. A few major hurdles also had to be jumped before we could happily settle down to the upcoming nuptials. The first was the invitations. I said it was completely up to Alex and Steve who they invited and naturally she wanted all her aunties to be there with their partners to which I had no objection.

We had one or two problems along the way with Alex's dress. She had to change the original shop which she had initially chosen but the dress she ended up with was breathtaking. Alex is a very slim size six and she chose a beautiful white dress with a strapless top covered in sequins. The bottom half was full length tulle again covered in sequins with a long train.

She had an elegant tiara with a full-length veil with very discreet sequins dotted around it Her bridesmaids all wore a dark cerise strapless dress with a panelled top and all looked incredible.

Alex wanted a 'hen do' and the new style of hen party is completely different from my day. Every one of my friends who had been married had enjoyed a night out either on their last day at work or a couple of days before the ceremony. The men I knew had all hit the town the night before, with many standing at the altar the next day looking deathly pale or green. Amy, who was chief bridesmaid, obviously had scoured the internet and come up with a well-priced weekend in Barcelona. Denise and I were invited along with Alex's future mother-in-law, Jean and baby Ryder, who was six months old at the time. Alex also invited six of her friends.

We had an uneventful flight over on one of the budget airlines and got a taxi to the pre-booked apartment. When we arrived, the place was a hovel. It was in the seediest part of town and nothing at all like the pictures online. There was no way we could stay there. It stank and looked unsafe. Luckily for us, one of Alex's friends had Spanish parents. She is fully fluent in the language and could tell the host that the place was unacceptable. Denise had already had visions of booking herself into a hotel. Eventually, eleven women of varying ages piled into a minibus and were driven to a better apartment. It still wasn't a penthouse overlooking the harbour with gold taps and marble fittings, but it was OK—just. We had to climb eight flights of stairs with a baby and a pram and worst of all there was no air conditioning, which was pretty poor in Barcelona in the summer. We found rooms for ourselves with Denise and me sharing. Over the next few days, we drank and partied day and night. We ate at some lovely restaurants on Los Rambles, in one of which I found myself standing up and singing 'Nessun Dorma' a cappella after a couple of large wines. Tourists stopped and watched, and a small crowd gathered around the restaurant's seating area. When I finished everyone erupted into cheers and applauded me. When I sat down the girls were all laughing at the sheer madness of the moment. To our delight we got a free bottle of wine for the table. It is one of my favourite moments.

The following day we also went out on a private yacht into the harbour. It was an absolute scorcher of a day. Denise loves the sun as long as she is in the shade, and she was almost melting. I got into my costume and enjoyed the rays as we bobbed up and down on the Mediterranean. Everyone went for a swim in the sea except Denise and I, and of course Ryder. Still to come that evening was an unexpected surprise for Alex.

Her Spanish-speaking friend Katie, and Amy had arranged to have waiters for a party they organised at the apartment. When they arrived I thought, *Oh hello…!*

The gentlemen waiters came into the apartment and nipped into the bathroom to get ready. When they emerged, I was soon scarlet. They had only the tiniest pieces of underwear on and a Dickie Bow – both in black silk. For the next couple of hours the waiters served us drinks and entertained us with impromptu dances and routines. Denise was petrified they might accidentally rub up against her or attempt to do a lap dance in front of her. She took it in good spirit and joined in with everything. She said loudly; "I hope you are going to put a coat on when you leave, you'll catch your death." We all remembered that trip with such lovely memories.

I have to say as well that these two guys were two of the sexiest-looking Spaniards I have ever seen. If I hadn't been old enough to be their mother, I don't think they would have stood a chance. They were exactly the type of guy I would have gone for in my youth. Foreign gents always took a shine to me as well when I was in my twenties—but that's a whole different book!

We had a few weeks to wait after we came back from Barcelona, to get the last of the wedding preparations out of the way. It all seemed to slot into place easily and before we knew it the day had arrived. Alex had stayed at Denise's the night before where we all enjoyed pizza and lots of laughter.

The morning of the wedding saw Denise making bacon sandwiches for everyone and pouring glasses of Bucks Fizz. Alex had her hair and make-up done. She was so serene and contented while the rest of us were buzzing with excitement. The flowers turned up late and were missing some of the promised blooms. That made me unhappy so required speedy fixing by the florist. My friend, Adam, had done Alex's hair and everything went to plan and did so for the entire day. Brian turned up on time looking lovely in his morning suit. He was going to accompany Alex in the vintage open-topped Rolls Royce that Steve had ordered. The car was a stunning, white model with red leather seating. She looked resplendent as she drove from Denise and Tom's house. I wore a pale pink two-piece suit with a large-brimmed hat in black.

As we approached the church in St Anne's, we could hear the bells ringing and outside St Joseph's were lots of people cheering. Some were in the grounds of the church. I am not entirely sure how members of the public knew that our family would be there. I know that at lots of weddings, people, usually women, stop to have a look at the bride entering, but this was different. There were so many of them calling out, "Hello Anne," "Hello Denise" – "Nice to see you Anne." I was chuffed. I didn't even mind some of them taking pictures. It's a lovely feeling when people in our area still have a fondness for us after all this time.

It was such a beautiful service. All my family and friends arrived for that magical day. After the wedding mass I made my way upstairs at the back of the church to an area where the choir sang. The church had provided me with the services of their organist and I sang Gounod's *Ave Maria.* The whole church gave me a stirring round of applause as I walked down the stairs to take my seat again. I had to wipe away the tears. It was such an emotional moment. Hopefully for everyone else too. That is what can happen in a church sometimes. Those few moments when you are watching or listening when something takes you over.

Vinny was a little star with his role of carrying the rings. His mum and dad were glowing with pride. The photographer was a really bubbly woman who spoke to everyone as though she had known them all their lives. She took some gorgeous pictures outside the church and while they went to the beach to take more pictures, we all headed to the reception venue.

The Grand Hotel is very plush. Alex and Steve had booked a room for themselves that night and the newlyweds had provided a welcome drink for their guests as they arrived. Most people knew each other and were happily chatting and drinking while a saxophonist and pianist played love songs in the ante room. Those who wanted a second drink were quick to point out that the prices at the bar were scandalous. I later learned that some of the younger guests made a quick trip to a supermarket and bought a bottle of vodka, hiding it in one, unnamed lady's bag. I can't say if I approve of that sort of thing, but some of the youngsters really were struggling when two gin and tonics were about £15. The waitress in charge of the staff spotted that one table were only drinking coke and water. She kept an eye on them and, sure as night follows day, she caught them out. The guilty party claimed that she had in fact only a bottle of water in her bag. Her pleas of innocence fell on deaf ears as the staff member pointed out that all the tables had been given complimentary water. It takes all sorts to make a wedding.

From left: Amy, my ex-husband Brian, Alex, Steve Palmer (son in law) and me.

The food was excellent, and the speeches had everyone in stitches. Steve's best man, Michael Swift, or 'Swifty' as everyone knows him, read all the cards with lovely messages from people who couldn't be at the wedding. Just before he concluded he read a card from me wishing Steve and Alex a lovely time on their honeymoon in Barcelona. They were absolutely amazed as they hadn't actually booked a honeymoon yet. I had booked them a weekend in Barcelona as a surprise wedding present from Denise, Tom and me. They were thrilled and the joy on their faces made it all worthwhile. Steve and Alex had the idea of giving a shout out to lots of people and they had bought gifts for those who had helped out in some way or other. It was like a mini awards ceremony as people were called to the top table to receive theirs, but it was a lovely touch.

After the formalities were over, the entire top table stood by the door to the next room and shook everyone's hand or gave them a kiss. Alex and Steve had chosen the Westlife song 'This love is Unbreakable' as their first dance and it was so emotional watching my little girl dancing for the first time as a married woman with her new husband.

At ten o'clock they served bacon and sausage butties, and we then danced some more. As the evening drew to a close, I was sitting at a table with Maureen, Denise and Linda and, even though we were still not really speaking, it was a step in the right direction for myself and Linda. I missed having her in my life, anyone who knows Linda will know that she is the life and soul of a party and can talk to anyone. Even as a child Linda wasn't shy. When she was six years old she would sing 'Hey Big Spender' by Shirley Bassey, that's a testament to Linda's character. I was so glad she made it for Alex and Steve's big day; it meant a lot to me that she was there. As for Coleen, this was around the time she was heading into the Celebrity Big Brother house for the first time. I think she was away with Ray and Ciara which is why she wasn't at the wedding. I did miss Coleen not being there, we all did.

The band had asked Bernie to sing and as usual, without any hesitation, she got up to sing. She had chatted with the band about how they might busk her chosen song beforehand. In fact she sang a great deal better than most singers on their best day. She performed the Sam Brown hit 'Stop', which she sings with such intensity and feeling. Even if we had not been aware of her diagnosis, her singing would bring a tear to your eye. Under the circumstances it was hard to take and the four of us sitting at the table became very tearful. We whispered to each other that it was so cruel. Hardly anyone in the room knew that Bernie had recently had the bombshell news. We looked at Erin and agreed how hard it would be for Bernie to handle, when, in all likelihood, she wouldn't be making these arrangements for her daughter. Weddings are emotional and usually for all the right reasons. It didn't mar any second of the day, it was just a part of it.

Looking at us on that table, to all intent and purpose we were as close now as we had ever been. The final song to be played that night was 'All You Need is Love' by the Beatles. What a joy it was to see Alex goofing around with a geeky dance to the song. To this day everyone says it was the best wedding they have ever been to and I think it was worth every penny. It turns out that the harmony our family were enjoying that day was masking what was about to emerge only a few days later.

Chapter 8

In The Mood One Last Time

On the day of Alex & Steve's wedding someone let slip to some of the guests that my sisters were getting back together to embark on another tour. This time it would be The Nolans farewell tour and that they would finish it by playing their last night at Wembley Stadium, a venue in which the act had never had the chance to perform. It was going to be called *'In The Mood One Last Time'*.

Word began to filter back to us within days of the nuptials and it was not what I was expecting to hear. I spoke to Maureen and said I would never fall out with my sisters again about anything but that if the press asked me why I wasn't doing this tour I would be truthful and say because I wasn't asked again.

By now Bernie had decided to tell the public that she had an incurable, but treatable, cancer. The revolutionary drug that she had been set to trial had to be cancelled. She had taken the drug once and within seconds of it being administered she was violently ill.

She was still carrying out her role in the musical, only taking time off when she had appointments. She had celebrated her birthday in Belfast in the October and asked to be released from her part when the show hit Derry. It was during that time that she wanted to go public. She had told a couple of people from the show, but the cast and crew were still in the dark. She wrote to them before she gave her interview to a newspaper. The news broke when the online edition of the papers went out the night before. All at once she was in demand from every news agency, magazine, TV and radio station in the country. She had to make her own choice as to who she was going to speak to and all those who had been rejected soon began beating a path to the rest of the family's door. They called and called wanting statements and interviews, but we all refused, closing ranks behind her.

On the flip side I was furious that she was going on tour with Maureen, Linda and Coleen again. I thought that the whole point of doing the first tour was to earn enough money that they would never have to work again?

If you have made that sort of money and love to tour then that is understandable. Let's face it Madonna and Cher keep on touring, and they have made millions. I knew though that Maureen in particular, hated being away from her son Danny and her granddaughter. She had been flogging her guts out for years on touring shows. She had worked in London's West End for two years living at a cousin's house for a year and the other with Bernie. She hardly ever came home even for the Sunday she had off and missed her husband Richie as well. She had appeared on TV giving interviews and knew that by doing a second tour she would risk us all falling out again, something I was aware she was keen to avoid at all costs. I knew that if she had made the money she had been hoping for, she would not do this new tour. I anxiously awaited the news.

Amy had decided that the time was right for her son's christening, and we were all excited. She went to church regularly and it was what she wanted. She was no longer with Ryder's dad but he was happy to take part. His family are from a different faith but he didn't have any objections to Ryder being christened as a Catholic. Amy chose St Cuthbert's church in Blackpool and sorted out the catering and venue at the West Coast Café in Blackpool.

Bernie made the journey north for the event. Amy had invited all her aunties along and everyone except Coleen could come which was great. Despite all the damage the argument had caused, she loved them all. The Mass itself was gorgeous. The priest on this occasion was Polish, and a gentle soul. My nephew Jake and my cousin Sandra' son, Alan, were to be Ryder's godfathers. Jake and his band at the time,

Rixton, sang the Bob Dylan classic 'Forever Young'. It was so beautiful and so emotional.

Bernie commented to me that it was a day tinged with sadness as she would not in all likelihood be able to see Erin do all this when she started a family.

After the christening we made our way into Blackpool town centre to the reception where Amy had pulled all the stops out and had put on a really good buffet. Most people were happy to mingle and chat but I looked across the room and saw that Bernie and Linda were standing next to the bar with Brian. Maureen came and sat with Denise, my aunty and me and had some food. No doubt she too sensed the divide, but nothing was said. It looked like this was going to be the way things were likely to be from now on. No one seemed to be able to get over the final hurdle and push for us all to make up.

Over the next few days the tour thing was still hanging over all our heads. We knew that it had been agreed, it was just the confirmation from my sisters that hadn't been forthcoming.

As always with this kind of thing, the news spreads rapidly. Denise and I challenged the girls to find out if it was true. They were already back working in shows up and down the country so when could they find time to do another tour? Maureen did confirm to me that dates were pencilled in for the following October.

Bernie had signed up to appear in panto and I had the chance to see her just before she went into it. I could see that something wasn't right. She had a cough that was quite persistent. It sounded quite tickly and she kept excusing herself saying how annoying it was. I thought it was strange that she was going into something as gruelling as a panto. By the time Christmas came my aunty was really upset about Bernie. She was perfectly well aware of Bernie's cancer, but it distressed her to find out that Bernie had pulled out of her show. It had become impractical for her to carry on while coughing. Singing was impossible. It was the first time that Bernie had ever pulled out of a show due to ill health. She had heard from her sisters that they had now rescheduled the dates on the tour for February as they were aware that her voice might not hold up. Bernie's illness was affecting her in so many ways and it was crushing for all of the family to see her this way.

I went to the *Sunday People*, to do an interview where I talked about the row and about Bernie's illness. I never apologised, but I did say that I regretted going to a newspaper and blamed the reason on my hurt and anger. It looked like I was backing down. I think to a certain extent I was. I'd had enough of the fighting. Denise was hurt at what I had said, which I totally understood. She wasn't pleased at some of the words that were used but I couldn't help how I felt. Bernie was terminally ill and I couldn't keep up the argument any longer. After doing that piece I felt a sense of calm that I had cleansed myself of the demons.

It didn't help a while later when Coleen did another piece saying she still wasn't speaking to us and that she felt the same way as she had at the time. Even though we had made up with the others, it seemed that there was still a divide.

The four Nolans, who were all set to tour in February, now decided to cancel it completely. Bernie was in no way fit enough to undertake such a gruelling tour.

That Christmas, Linda, Maureen and Richie went to Weybridge to spend the holiday with Bernie and some of our Irish relatives flew over to have Christmas with them.

Denise was appearing in pantomime in Surrey that year and offered her house in Blackpool to use as she has a large dining room. She surprised us by turning up on Christmas Eve and we thought they were crazy making such a journey for one night and a day.

The house was once again full of laughter, music and love. We all had a lot to be thankful for really and made a conscious effort not to discuss the upcoming tour. After dinner we went into the lounge where a small mountain of presents was waiting to be unwrapped. Denise and I handed out gifts. Those people who were away had all left their presents with

Denise and we had given our presents for everyone to Maureen to take to Bernie's house.

Watching Christmas TV is one of our favourite things to do on Christmas Day evening. We watched an Andy Williams Christmas Show and then out came *It's A Wonderful Life* which has to be our all-time number-one Christmas Movie. Aunty Teresa fell asleep a couple of times, gently snoring in the armchair. We washed the dishes and cleared the rubbish away. The house was a hive of activity with people either watching TV or playing games with the young ones. I can't think of any time of year that is better than Christmas.

For New Year I went down to Broxbourne where Denise was still in panto and it was lovely to see her. Amy came along too with Ryder. It was his first panto and he didn't take a bit of it in. Ryder couldn't be more different than Vinny just as adorable but in a different way. He certainly had a great set of lungs on him that was for sure.

Chapter 9

Goodbye! Too Much to Say

2013

We were told in January 2013 that Bernie was not in the best of health. She had enjoyed a holiday in Italy and, upon returning, her throat was painful. She still had the persistent cough and when she spoke it was very breathy. She whispered more than she spoke. The doctors had intervened saying surgery was possible, but that it wasn't without risks and might even be fatal. She declined the operation and opted for injections and the use of a speech therapist. She was told round about that time that she would never sing again. All our family love to sing, not only on stage for a living, but while we are doing housework or making a cup of tea. Whenever there is a party, the karaoke usually ends up being switched on. It's always been there. The fact that we all like the same music is a blessing. We all have our favourites of course: I am crazy about Barbra Streisand; Maureen and Brian love Jack Jones. Denise is a total Sinatra addict, as are we all. Bernie loved all the standards that we as a family grew up listening to. She also liked soul and more funky stuff like Earth Wind and Fire and George Benson.

When you have been a professional singer all your life, music runs through every part of your DNA. When you are preparing to record an album you listen to demo tracks. You learn new songs for live shows and when you are in the company of musicians you hear new and old music all the time. We would sit and discuss music that casual listeners might not engage with. We would talk about little known musicians who had popped up on albums. Then we would chat about musical terms and how good so and so sounds when they use their chest voice or that it sounds better in their head voice. We would talk about octaves and harmonies in the same was as some people talk about their shopping.

I don't sing professionally nearly as much as I used to, but if I was told I couldn't sing any more I would be crushed. So, trying to get into how Bernie was feeling when hearing that wasn't easy. I don't think she ever gave up her fight against cancer and she had done all that was expected of her by the medics, and more. But it seemed that for every forward step she took, she was knocked back three. The fact that she was so far away in Weybridge was also an obstacle but we were all delighted when Bernie told us she was making the journey north to spend Steve's birthday weekend in Blackpool. In the end it was a traumatic weekend that is etched on my mind. For a few days we thought we had lost her.

Both Steve and Linda have birthdays in February, so they decided to make the journey and celebrate both days. For Steve's on the 19th it had been pretty normal. It was obvious that Bernie wasn't in perfect health. Her hair was wispy since she had lost quite a lot of it during her treatment and she was still coughing and quite breathless, but her indomitable spirit pushed through this and she was on good form. She had stumbled outside the restaurant where about twenty-five people had attended. Our aunty was upset that they had chosen the restaurant that they had because it was on the first floor. She was in a wheelchair and could only walk very slowly for a few yards. She was definitely unable to climb a full flight of stairs. The staff had been sympathetic but could not accommodate her needs.

Bernie was fighting hard, but we knew that she was not winning the battle. Aunty Teresa took comfort that she would see Bernie over the next few days. She was still not on great terms with Linda or Coleen so she would miss out on that celebration too. As it happened, Bernie didn't feel well at Steve's birthday meal and ended up in our local hospital. Tests indicated that, even with her bucketload of problems, she was not in any immediate danger. She took things easy for the next few days and headed to the restaurant for Linda's birthday meal.

They left quite early as Bernie was ill once more. That night she took a turn for the worse and ended up once again, in the hospital. This time though the same tests showed that blood was not getting the necessary oxygen and that thing were looking pretty desperate. Steve was told that they were looking at an 'end of life situation' and as one would expect, he was broken. He had to tell Bernie that she was likely to die imminently. He then texted the whole family the dreadful news. She was given drugs that rallied her and it was suggested that she be moved to a hospice.

Family members came to see her over the next few days. The Trinity Hospice was a great idea because it was roomy with no restrictions on visiting. They even agreed to allow us to have little parties with alcoholic drinks. The staff there were fantastic with us. However, because the hospital and hospice had none of Bernie's notes, they had assumed the end-of-life situation. They hadn't seen her in the days previously when she was in relatively good health. When they spoke to Bernie's main care provider, they had a much clearer picture. Their initial diagnosis was that she had a pulmonary embolism but after further tests, including a scan, they determined Bernie was suffering from lymphangitis which was the result of the cancer spreading and they could treat this condition with drugs—even more drugs for her to take. She was already on anti-cancer drugs, morphine, methadone and now steroids to help stop swelling. So their discussion about Bernie dying was slightly premature. She had headaches and her vision was blurred but she was still alert enough to engage with us all. Her speech was very hushed and she was slurring her words, which was distressing for us all to see. We all tried to make conversation as light and casual as we could.

Bernie stayed in Blackpool for a few more days, improving each day and she regained some of her strength. Steve was totally dedicated to her and slept in the guest bed next to her every night. One day all the sisters gathered together with Bernie and we chatted and laughed about all our lives. Bernie must have known that her time was limited and said to me, "Anne, I want to talk to you about the tour."

I brushed it aside and told her that it didn't matter, that it wasn't important.

"We really don't need to Bernie," I said.

She waved her hand letting me know that she wanted to say something.

"No, I wanted to say that you should have been on that tour. We were wrong."

I made it clear once more that it didn't matter, but the words had gone deeper than I thought they would. She had vindicated me. She had known that leaving me out was wrong. She didn't apologise to me, and she didn't need to. It must have been on her mind for some time, and she wanted to make sure that I knew. That meant a lot to me. Particularly as she had said it in front of my other sisters, and they heard it.

The fact that all six of us were together that day put everything into perspective. It was what I had always wanted all my life. OK, we had great successes as the Nolans, more success than we could have ever hoped or dreamed of. Also, we had enjoyed success as solo artistes. Bernie, Denise and I had all recorded albums. It had been fine that the act had faded away. People were perfectly entitled to have a go at a solo career. What we had said in countless interviews over the years was that there had never been any pressure on any of us to stay in the group.

Denise had left first and she famously said, "I'm leaving the act, not the family."

We all gave her our blessing. I too had left the act and then re-joined it after I found I missed the work and needed the money. They had never barred me from being one of the group members. Even years later when *Loose Women* invited us onto the show to perform we did so as a five-piece act. All I ever wanted was for us to enjoy our careers and still be that huge, crazy family. Despite the terrible, tragic events unfolding now, we were at last a united family again.

Whilst Bernie was in the hospice her house was burgled. Their friend had called them and told them their TV had been nicked together with some jewellery. They had prised open a box that contained photographs of their stillborn baby, Kate. It also had treasured items in there like her hospital wristband and, fortunately, they hadn't damaged those. The things that had been stolen could be replaced. We will never know if she was burgled because the thieves knew she was in Blackpool because of press coverage. Nevertheless, it was a despicable thing to do and I hope the scum who did it know who they did it to and that guilt rests heavily on their minds.

While Bernie was still in Blackpool we were able to see her almost every day. She had started wearing baseball caps, and her wig if she went to a restaurant. On St Patrick's Day, we all piled up and went to a lovely restaurant that overlooks the River Wyre estuary. She was able to see all her nieces and nephews as well as the grown-ups. We had a photo taken with us all dressed in those big foam leprechaun's hats. I can understand her determination to go home to Weybridge, but that didn't stop me from not wanting her to go. We all knew that her time was limited and that makes every hour much more precious.

I can't put into words properly what kind of feeling you get when you know that the person in front of you who is chatting away and laughing is not going to be there for much longer. You are caught between feeling such pity for them and your own selfish feelings that you don't want them to go. Heaven knows what the person must be feeling.

We are all going to die at some point, but when we think about that we are thinking years away, and at a time when we probably aren't expecting it. Knowing it can come at any point must have been terrifying for her. As much as she had resigned herself to the fact, she must have had so many things on her mind. Not seeing her daughter grow up, not being able to take part in all the things we all take for granted. Fear must have been there as well as sadness, bitterness and anger. I now look at that photo and see that her smile was only for the camera and for us to cherish. Inside she must have felt desperate.

Bernie went home to Weybridge shortly afterwards, but not without planning her funeral to the very last detail. She had chosen the venue, the words and even the coffin. It must have been the worst thing she had to do. She wrote a letter to us and an open letter to be read at her funeral. Bernie was not in the least bit religious so there would be no faith element to her funeral. She also wished to be cremated and laid to rest next to her stillborn baby, Kate. We had no idea how long she had left when she set off home. When she gave an interview to the press saying she had gone home to live out her final days with her family, I was devastated.

As much as everything that goes on around you, you still have to try to live your own life. Brian, my brother, had often said, "What is wrong with our family? Why do we have so much bad luck?"

I countered him and disagreed. Any large family is going to have lots of things that happen to it. Yes, on the face of it you could say it was bad luck, but we have had lots of good luck too. It's just that it was not following us around right now.

At this time my Aunty Teresa had noticed some spots on her arm. They were like freckles but a reddish brown and blue colour. A trip to her own GP in March followed. He was not happy with the look of them and talked to her about there being a possibility it was melanoma and that she would have to undergo further tests. Although she was approaching eighty, I have to say that she was very stoical about the inconvenience of hospital visits and tests. She would undergo blood tests, a biopsy and goodness knows what else. Maureen and I have cars, and she called on the services of Brian and his wife, Annie, to get to any appointments. This wasn't much of an inconvenience as the appointments were all local. Aunty Teresa didn't seem unduly concerned even when more of the freckles began to appear. It was starting to look like someone had got a fountain pen and flicked it on her arm. Two weeks passed and Aunty was told that she had skin cancer.

We hadn't told Bernie about it as we didn't see any point in giving her something else to worry about. My Aunty Teresa listened carefully to what the doctors told her but it came as a body blow when they told her the cancer was also incurable. In her case, because of her age, it was considered to be very slow progressing. They gave her all the talks about living with cancer and told her about the available treatments. Chemotherapy was not an option but radiation was. For now, they wanted to remove two of the larger tumours that they thought were particularly troubling. Aunty talked about it as if they were taking a pimple off. She didn't flinch when they said she would need a skin graft, with skin taken from her outer thigh.

On the arranged date she went to the hospital and had the minor operation. I know they have to do what is necessary, but I had no concept of what a big chunk of her forearm they were going to remove. It looked like a shark had got hold of her. They grafted the skin and put her a small dressing on the site. The day after the operation a few of us went for a meal at our local Sizzler and she was absolutely fine. She said the graft had caused her a little bit of discomfort, but other than that, she felt no pain. They had also taken samples out of a few other tumours to test the level of malignancy and removed one of the other growths giving her a couple of stitches. She was remarkable.

Her own mood was very low, not because of her own cancer, but because of Bernie. She would often say, "I don't care about me; they can take me instead of Bernie."

It was so heart breaking. Our Aunty Teresa had been like a second mother to us all. She had never had children of her own, but I can tell you for a fact, she had a mother's bond and instinct with every one of us. The grandchildren all adored her too. She has a kind face and the biggest heart. She had suffered in her own life too. Her husband, Jim, had died only a few years before and then my mum. Those two sisters were in complete unison on just about everything. They shared the same sense of humour and were the very best of friends. She even called our mum, Mum. Watching her sister die with Alzheimer's was crushing for her. Her own body had been punished too with arthritis, and yet she never complained about having to use a wheelchair or scooter. She had supported me during my cancer ordeal and then Linda. Now in such a selfless way she was wishing to exchange her own life so Bernie could live.

Aunty Teresa was referred to the specialist cancer unit at Preston. They practically knew all our family by now. She really got along with her surgeon and he offered her a revolutionary new way of delivering controlled chemotherapy injected directly into her arm. She was well aware that the results were not guaranteed and that there was a risk of some side effects such as sickness and a general feeling of not being well. She signed up for the treatment and it showed pretty instant results. Some of the lesions cleared up altogether in a matter of a few days. Others also receded during the weeks that followed. She was never told she could be cured, but it was something she was happy to endure.

Bernie had a couple of weeks in Weybridge where she was fairly comfortable but then she began to succumb to the ravages of the disease. She was in a great deal of pain only alleviated by super-strong morphine. Denise tried to visit her as much as she could and Steve was magnificent through all of it. He was nursing her and looking after the home and Erin. The two of them were really put through the most harrowing ordeal. As time went on, she grew weaker and spent much of her time asleep. The drugs had the effect of making her 'out of it' and that was, again, a good thing. When the time approached, it was decided we should all make our way to her house. When you are visiting someone you know is going to die it is frightening. Yes, Bernie and I had always had many differences, but she was still my little sister. I loved her as much as you could love anyone. I looked at her in her bed and in between her sleeps she had moments when she would wake up and smile to acknowledge us. We played music and watched her favourite films. Not that she was watching them, but I'm sure she was listening. We sang to her around the bed. When she rested, we sat together and ate a meal, reminiscing about our lives, which did bring a lot of comfort to us.

The end was fairly swift. She had been in unbelievable pain. When you leant over and gave her a feather-light kiss on the cheek, if you touched any part of her, she cried in pain. Turning her over to prevent her getting sore was also painful for her. I would have done anything to make her well again. To turn back the clocks. To remove the pain. Right up to the very last minute I kept thinking that I would wake up and it had been a horrible dream, or that she would suddenly revive and be cured. That didn't happen though. She died on July 4th. Our family were broken.

Within the hour of her dying, journalists were on the phone to my manager, and to Denise's to ask if we would all be attending the funeral. They wanted us to give an interview or make a statement. Denise went into a rage saying, "Give them this quote: Can they stoop any lower?"

We stayed a while to give Steve the support he needed. He quite rightly wanted time alone and so we left shortly afterwards and came home. I developed a coping mechanism without even realising it. On the journey home, I kind of blanked out what had happened. I began thinking, as I didn't see Bernie every day, she was still away touring. That barrier worked some of the time but at other times it didn't. I could be doing the most mundane thing and burst into tears. I had a lot to cry about; we all did. Not only the loss of Bernie, but for a talent wiped out, for a child who had lost her mother, and my own feelings about the lost time we had endured during the fall out. I don't blame anyone for the fall out—it just happened. A rough road lay ahead to get all our lives back on track.

I started to hear about the plans for Bernie's funeral. The Grand Theatre in Blackpool had been chosen as the venue. We have performed there in loads of Summer Seasons and pantomime as well as in charity events and touring productions. The theatre means so much to our family that it was the perfect choice. We would also have the necessary room for her many family members and friends. A list was drawn up of all the people who would be invited. Our friend Dave Creagan offered to act as doorkeeper. If he knew you then you would be fine; if not, he would check on the list.

As much as fans have been fantastic, we still wanted to have some level of privacy. We had a piece in the local newspaper inviting all those people who admired her as a performer to come and say their goodbyes outside the theatre. The management even offered to have staff with a book of condolences outside the foyer and to relay the audio outside on speakers. In the end, as well as the TV and radio stations that were covering the funeral, thousands, and I mean literally tens of thousands, of people had travelled from all across the country to pay their respects. We had messages from other show business people like Lorraine Kelly, Bucks Fizz, Jane McDonald and the stars of *Loose Women* and *This Morning*. Many of them had sent beautiful floral tributes. It was also announced on the RTE six o'clock news at home in Ireland.

Steve had worked closely with the people at the Grand as well as with my brother, Brian to work out some of the more intricate details. In the end, my goodness me… what a spectacle. I hope that doesn't make it sound trivial or as if it was some kind of jamboree, but it was such a fitting way to pay tribute to someone who had been in show business since she was two years old. Celebrities also came along, from *Coronation Street* cast members to Coleen's ex, Shane

Richie, Chubby Brown, Cannon and Ball and Roy Walker. Several cast members from *The Bill* and *Brookside*, where Bernie had made a lasting impression, also attended. Even the cast of *Chicago* came along in a show of support.

The whole theatre was packed, with the front two rows reserved for immediate family. As the guests gathered and took to their seats, tracks were played from Bernie's debut album. The songs were beautifully crafted and showed her flawless vocals. All the songs were emotional power ballads which only added to the intense, poignant atmosphere. The family had gathered earlier and we were to travel in cars with the funeral cortege. Some of the lads in the family wanted to be pall bearers and I have often thought since, that as well as being an honour to carry out the task, it is painful to have a loved one on one's shoulder. We walked into the theatre first.

The chatter stopped in an instant and all that could be heard were the sobs of my family. Then, my brothers Brian and Tommy along with Tommy Jnr and Maureen's husband, Richie, her son Danny, Steve and Shane followed, carrying Bernie onto the stage. It may seem a strange thing to do if you are not from a show business background, but I can tell you, there was no more fitting place on earth for Bernie to be, even in death, than centre stage in the country's most gorgeous theatre, in the town she grew up in and loved while being surrounded by people who loved her, with crowds outside who also adored her. If she was watching, and I am sure she was, she would be grinning from ear to ear saying how much she loved it.

As we made our way to our seats, Coleen spotted Aunty Teresa and came over to her and bent over to hug her. The two were inconsolable. In the years that Coleen was too young to join the group she stayed with Aunty back in Blackpool for some time, so it was only natural for them to support one another.

Denise and Coleen also hugged each other as they sobbed into each other's shoulders in a moment of grief that was felt by everyone. The actual service, if you can call it a service because, as I say, Bernie wasn't religious, was a moving experience. She had written a letter that she wanted to be read out so Maureen got up, stood on the stage, and delivered it word perfect. It was a miracle she was able to contain herself as she got the words out. The letter said,

"Hello everyone, and thanks for coming. Don't be crying too much for me, obviously I'd like a little bit. I think I am worth a little crying, but not too much. No one has had a better life than me, 50 years of singing in some of the best shows, Chicago, Blood Brothers, The Sound Of Music, My Fair Lady, The City Of Angels – What an amazing time I've had. By the time I was 19, I had been all over the world, sang with Stevie Wonder, toured with Frank Sinatra – I mean, do not mourn my passing, CELEBRATE my wonderful life. I have the most wonderful family who have supported me always giving

me great advice and constant love. As for my husband and daughter, how did I get so lucky?

Steve has been my constant rock, misunderstood sometimes terribly at times, but if only you knew what he has done for me and how he has set up Erin's life so that she won't ever have to worry again, how he has cared for me and basically given up so much for me. Every 17th October I want you to have a party or at least a good old drink for me – Make it a 'vodka mule'.

By the time it had been read everyone was in bits. Erin then made her way onto the stage to deliver the Elizabeth Frye poem *'Do Not Weep For Me'*. It seemed to be especially fitting. Erin did not break down at all. We were so proud that such a young girl could stand there and deliver such intense words in front of a thousand people and not break under the strain. The final touch was to show a video on a giant screen that covered almost the entire stage. The video showed Bernie singing a breathtaking version of the Whitney Houston track 'Run To You'. What gave it even more impact was that it had been filmed at one of Bernie's concerts. It had been her finale song and she both looked and sounded incredible. As she reached the final note the compere on the video who was actually my brother, Brian, could be heard saying things like;

"Ladies and Gentlemen, one more time, let's hear it for the incomparable… Miss Bernie Nolan."

Bernie would then run back on stage waving at us all, blowing kisses and saying, "Thanks". It was almost too much for everyone in the theatre to take.

As mourners left the theatre and headed to the crematorium, we slipped out of the stage door where the press had gathered as the coffin was placed in a stunning vintage hearse. We agreed to have photographs taken, which is not what most people have to go through. It felt weird standing in a line being photographed when your sister is in a coffin at the side of you. I think we were all on some kind of autopilot by then and just let them get on with it.

As we drove to the crematorium the streets were heaving with fans and well-wishers. Some threw single flowers onto the hearse and I saw people who had been moved to tears. People who didn't know Bernie but felt as though they did. To some extent they did know her. They had seen her on TV since she had been fourteen and on stage in Blackpool since she was two. They had watched her interviews, so they knew her character.

Once we arrived at the crematorium there were more words and Steve delivered a message saying how much Bernie had meant to everyone. I remember the line, "Incapable of malice," which seemed a fair summary. He invited people to come and touch the coffin as a final goodbye.

As we left the crematorium loads of doves were released, flying skywards. Everyone headed to the Grand Hotel for food and drinks to celebrate her life. Not a day goes by when I don't think about Bernie, yet life still goes on.

From that day onwards our family were mostly all speaking again. It was still a little strained between Denise and Coleen but things were getting better. We don't really talk about what split us up. There is no point; we all still have our opinions about why it happened but it's in the past and you can't change the past or predict the future, so I hope we all live in the present, learn from the past and hope for a happy and healthy future.

***

It was the end of September and Amy and I attended my niece Laura's 30th birthday party with the rest of the adults in the family.

Ryder was just over a year old at the time so his grandad, Brian, was looking after him at his home. I picked Ryder up after the party to take him home and his grandad said he had a little rash on the top of his back and a slightly raised temperature. The rash didn't look too bad and his temperature was not too high, so I gave him some Calpol and put him to bed.

The next day, however, his temperature was slightly raised and the rash was still there so Amy and I took him to A&E at Victoria Hospital just to have him checked out. They assured us at the hospital that everything looked OK but if he didn't improve to bring him straight back.

Things didn't improve; in fact, they got decidedly worse so the next morning we took him back to A&E where they did lots of tests but couldn't find out what was wrong so decided to keep him in overnight.

The next day his rash had worsened and his temperature was soaring. We were so worried about him and the medical staff were dumbfounded. The rash was now over most of his body, big red welts, and his eyes were almost closed. I remember picking him up in my arms and cradling him to sleep singing 'You are my sunshine, my only sunshine, you make me happy when skies are grey'. When I got to the line at the end of the song which is 'Please don't take my sunshine away', Amy and I burst into tears.

It was the middle of the week now and Amy spent the whole time at the hospital. I visited when I was allowed to as did his paternal grandma and all his aunts and uncles. His dad also visited whenever he could.

The staff were so baffled by his condition that he had been visited by numerous different members of staff, including students asking if they could see him and ask us some questions. We said that was fine as long as they didn't disturb him.

Then one day a doctor came to examine him and said he had a condition called Erythema Multiforme Major which can be fatal. The cause is unclear, but some cases are the result of a reaction to an infection or medicine. Once the condition had been diagnosed the doctors were able to treat it and Ryder recovered after one of the worst weeks of our lives.

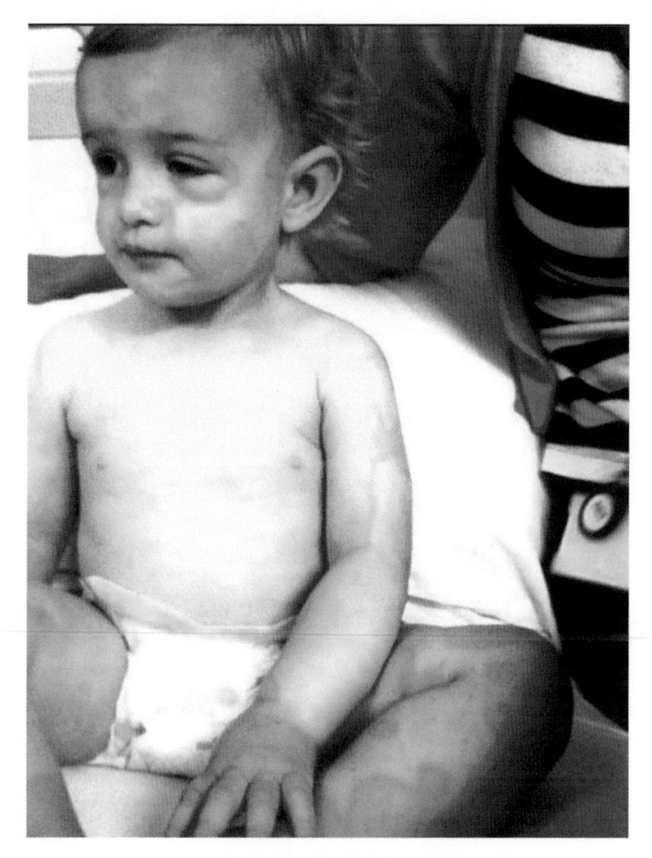

Ryder while ill in hospital

Chapter 10

Fly Me to the Moon

2014

It was a grey Christmas day in 1973. Eight very happy children and teens piled into the back of my dad's estate car and made the short journey from our house on Waterloo Road in Blackpool to the Cliffs Hotel on Northshore. My mum and dad had one golden rule and that was that we never worked on Christmas Day. However, this year it would prove to be different. The Cliffs Hotel was one of Blackpool's most luxurious hotels at the time. A large, beautiful, red-brick building peering over the Irish Sea. A hotel that our parents definitely wouldn't have been able to afford with all us kids. The manager of the hotel asked my dad if we would perform for their Christmas luncheon for the residents. My dad declined their offer and thanked them for the opportunity. However, they came back again a couple of days later and my dad again said no but thanked them. On the third attempt, in a form of retaliation, my dad gave them a fee that was way out of The Singing Nolans range, thinking that will keep them quiet and they won't ask again after that, but they did. So, the golden rule was broken for this very special occasion and it was a gig that would change our lives for ever.

As we arrived in the hotel, we made our way into the function room. There was a wonderful sense of Christmas cheer with guests wearing paper hats from the Christmas crackers and laughing could be heard as I opened the brass handle into the room. I wrote about this in my first book but, as a reminder, when we came off stage my dad was approached by a smart man who asked if he could speak to him for a few moments. My mum, however, was not impressed as she wanted to get home and check on the turkey and ham (a very Irish tradition to have both). As my dad spoke to this man, we were all sitting round a big circular table which was draped in a white linen cloth. The younger girls were drinking bottles of pop as a special treat for the day's work. As my dad returned to the table, he told of a deal that the mysterious man had offered him: he wanted to bring the family to London to perform in his new club on Drury Lane called The London Rooms.

The venue was a plush, expensive dining cabaret type of room where we would sing to diners from all over the world. Our brothers didn't want to leave Blackpool and live in London, so they stayed in Blackpool and the rest of the family moved to London and that is when The Nolan Sisters started. Now four decades later, it is believed that the gentleman's net worth is estimated at $6 billion… BILLION.

His portfolio of companies consists of more than 200 companies in fifteen countries. They include Tottenham Hotspur Football Club, property, hotels and restaurants. When we first signed up to his company, we went to London and moved into Joe Lewis's mansion while we found a home of our own. Joe and his wife Esther really looked after us. We had never stayed in accommodation like that in our lives. He had tennis courts and a private swimming pool and I got on especially well with his daughter, Vivienne.

Fast forward almost forty years. I received a call at home from Vivienne, she had got in touch with my management and asked if they would put us in touch. Her voice hadn't changed at all and it was lovely to reconnect with her. We chatted about the old times and she told me that her Dad, Joe, had always kept abreast of what we were doing and that he had read my first book. He thought that I had been through quite a bit and that he would like to treat me to a holiday. Not only was I going on the holiday but could take up to five people with me. I had no idea where the holiday might take us.

When I had chosen who was to come with me, I had to email Vivienne and tell her their names. The plan I had would be to take all my sisters with me, but as I didn't have a choice with dates, understandably, when I approached my sisters with the dates in question they were all working away.

After considering who I could take, I chose Amy and Ryder, my best friend Jacqui, my other friend

Celia, and my cousin and all-round barrel of laughs, Angie, who could make Gadhafi cry laughing. She has been a great friend as well as cousin who had stuck by me throughout all the horrors of the argument.

Shortly afterwards the email arrived with details of the holiday. Firstly, we were to fly to Florida on Virgin Atlantic and once there we would drive to a smaller airfield nearby. There we would board Joe's private jet and fly to Nassau in the Bahamas.

Joe was providing us with one of the villas on this luxury resort. Amy was straight online to find more details about the resort. She found out that Joe had built this luxury resort in the Bahamas with exclusive villas and apartments that were available as permanent homes or holiday rentals. One of the joint owners was Tiger Woods!

I was certain that when we got there we would have a small apartment and was so excited. It was really tough for some of my family who would normally been going with us. Denise was away herself and Maureen, Coleen and Linda were working while Alex was pregnant and couldn't fly. When the date arrived for us to go, I could hardly contain my excitement. We had great seats and service with Virgin. As I said earlier, I am not the best of fliers, but this trip was a little out of the ordinary. Even though I had flown to many places in the world, I had never fully got used to it.

Anyway, the flight went without a hitch. We were met at Orlando by a driver employed by Joe, who took us in a limousine to the small airfield. The aircraft was delayed for an hour so I had no idea what it looked like. When it roared into view it was a sight to see. It even had a personalised registration! We boarded and I have to tell you – this was not like Ryanair and even the Virgin Atlantic's first-class lounge was a very poor relation.

From left: Anne, Vivienne Lewis, Celia Garside, daughter Amy, best friend Jacqui Bloom, Cousin Angie Ganly and grandson Ryder.

As the limousine pulled up outside this private jet we were met by the pilots who wore uniforms like all pilots do and standing next to him was our own personal steward! As I climbed the steps for this once-in-a-lifetime opportunity, I took a moment and looked back at the airfield almost as if I was the USA First Lady boarding Air Force One. Taking a deep breath, in sheer amazement, and feeling the warm air rush through my hair, it was a moment I'll never forget.

We sat in luxurious white leather armchairs and rested our feet on sumptuous cream carpets. Where on long flights you sometimes have a screen in the back of the seat in front of you, we had a huge flat screen TV on the wall. I cannot describe the standard of luxury. The woodwork was all highly polished walnut, finished with chrome. Mood lighting gave the aircraft the final polish.

With cousin Angie

We had the conventional flight safety demonstration before take-off and once we were airborne we were free to move about the cabin and sit at the tables or lounge on the plush sofas. The flight was only a couple of hours but we were given exquisite food and drink and treated like Royalty.

Once we arrived in Nassau, we were driven by a chauffeur who took us to the resort itself. I don't think I have ever seen a resort that was so elegant. The layout of the place was like a village. Some of the houses were on the beachfront and others in small avenues that entwined around picturesque palm trees and flower gardens. There was a central club that housed the reception, restaurants, shops and other facilities. There were three huge swimming pools, one with a lazy river; another had a gigantic children's swimming area with play blocks, ropes and slides. Finally, there was an infinity pool for adults only with spectacular views over the Atlantic Ocean.

Although we were staying in the Bahamas, this resort was on Providence Island. The whole complex is 600 acres of some of the finest properties in the world. If you take a look online, look for the 'Albany, Bahamas'. We were all open-mouthed at the sheer elegance of the place as we arrived.

Not a thing was out of place anywhere, from immaculately manicured lawns to fine dining and spa facilities. This place had the lot – in shed loads. Our own villa was located on the beach. I say 'villa' but that is doing it an injustice. It is a mansion and the house Joe Lewis himself lives in when he is not on his yacht.

We had a bedroom each and each person had a drawing room, a bathroom and a dressing room. We had a dining room that you could hold a dance in and a kitchen so large that I commented I had played in smaller rooms with my sisters! Each bedroom was like an average-sized lounge. Outside, we had our own private pool and loungers. The list just kept getting longer. We were then introduced to our staff!

We had a cook, a cleaner, waiter and maid. We even had someone to do the food shopping for us. All that kitchen space and we never had to cook a meal. Outside there was a barbeque that was manned whenever we wanted it. We never had to lift a finger. It didn't take any of us any time at all to get used to the place. Amy made several new friends on the first night but, sadly, they were not human. They came in the shape of mosquitos that thought she was the perfect specimen to have a feast on. All of us were bitten to an extent, but none of us like Amy. The weather was glorious with barely a cloud in the sky. I can't think of a more perfect location anywhere on earth. When it came to going into the main town in Nassau to have a look around, we found we had been given the services of a driver!

We enjoyed lazy days by the different pools and evenings at the restaurants. Ryder really loved the play pool and we enjoyed spending time with him. We even went in our own pool late at night, with Jacqui fulfilling her long-held ambition of skinny dipping. I wanted to but I didn't dare, apart from the fact that I am not a great swimmer.

Joe Lewis had left us to our own devices for the whole time we were there.

About halfway through the holiday we were given an invitation to his yacht. You may have heard about it; it is reported to have cost $150 million and had recently undergone a $65 million refit. It is more than 300 foot long, has seven decks and is used as Joe's floating home and office. The invitation for dinner was extended to all of us. We did our hair and make-up and wore our best clothes.

As we were driven there I had butterflies. We were welcomed as long-lost friends and escorted around the yacht. Joe has a private collection of artworks which is stunning. I mean, genuine Picassos (not the posters you used to buy in Athena!). He had Matisse, Lucian Freud and Henry Moore pieces and sculptures by Francis Bacon – it was insane. The most incredible thing for me was that on the plane coming from England we watched a movie called *The Woman In Gold* about a painting by Gustav Klimt called 'The Lady In Gold' and when we stepped onto Joe's ship the first thing we saw was that painting.

My lot being as they are, we got our phones out to take pictures but we were politely asked not take photographs while on board. Ryder was taken to the cinema with some staff who would keep him entertained while we ate. The food that night was to die for. Joe had no edge to him. He remembered all my sisters by their names and had nothing but kind words and funny, kind memories.

The evening went much too quickly. I don't mean that because of the setting, it would have been the same if we were sitting on orange boxes around a Calor gas fire in a caravan at Skegness. It was just great to hear stories that I had forgotten about and to tell him ones that he had also long since forgotten.

He had a real interest in Bernie and what she had been through and I could see he was genuinely saddened. We also talked about the Nolans after we left his company. Whilst he had moved onto much bigger things than the Hanover Grand Group, he had nothing but fondness for it.

We had left his company in 1978 and he sold it just a year later. I don't regret leaving; we had grown in popularity but were still on a salary when the decision to leave was made. Joe understood our reasons; he was a businessman, after all. If we were managing ourselves we could command a bigger fee and it would all be ours. Though I personally still have misgivings, some of the best work undertook was whilst working for his organisation. Some terrible decisions, mainly about our image and what we sang, had been taken on our behalf by people within the company. Nevertheless, the money was good for a group straight out of the northern working men's clubs. Joe had surrounded us with undoubtedly the best people. John Coleman and Alyn Ainsworth were the finest composers and arrangers Britain has ever had. Stuart Morris was absolutely unmatched in the UK as a TV producer. He had been head of the BBC's light entertainment department for several years and responsible for all the biggest TV shows in Britain. He had a ferocious temper and could reduce grown men to quivering wrecks. Stuart could be tough with us but he brought out our best. He always fought to make sure we had the best sound, musicians, and song arrangements. He got us onto TV programmes that would normally be impossible for unknowns like us. Cliff Richard's show was viewed by 22 million people and that was our TV debut – Yes, the whole series as Cliff's guests on Saturday night, prime time.

Similar figures viewed *The Two Ronnies* and even more tuned in to see Morecambe and Wise. We had Nigel Lythgoe as our choreographer, and the icing on the cake came via Stuart with the tours alongside Engelbert Humperdinck in America and all across Europe with Frank Sinatra. That kind of start doesn't happen to many people. Yes, we had to work like dogs. We were at the London Room every night and when we weren't there, we were touring the country. We recorded records and TV shows during the day and then went to work at night.

We had listened to the advice of people outside the industry who told us to wear ridiculous clothes off stage and on stage. We had our hair done how they thought it should be done. All of that brought negative press. It never reflected who we were as people. It was a tough apprenticeship, but I wouldn't have swapped a single moment of it. Joe Lewis was 99% responsible for that success. If we had stayed with him, would he have gone on to make us show business establishment and taken us Stateside? It might have worked, but then there was always the nagging feeling that more money was to be made by the act being outside the management stranglehold of Hanover Grand.

After the meal that night I went home feeling flushed from having drunk a little too much Champagne and cocktails. I was so elated, but reflective. There would be little chance of sleeping that night as I recalled all the things I had tried to take in without me looking like I was casing the joint. I went over and over the conversations in my mind. Joe still had that spark in his eye that had made him such a business giant. I was on a cloud that he had found time to find little old me and give me a taste of the high life. We were able to enjoy the last few days of the holiday in luxury whilst the mosquitos made more of a meal of all of us. Amy was to come home with a face like a page in a book in braille – but a very sun-tanned book.

Our return home was just as luxurious as the journey there. Driven in a limousine to the airport, the private jet to Florida and a flight with Virgin with hundreds of people much more like me. It was good while it had lasted!

Returning home, we tried to adjust to life in the slow lane. Work beckoned and babysitting duties continued. As I walked around Asda with a rattling trolley picking up washing powder and milk a week later, I realised I had been really lucky to have enjoyed that experience. That's the thing with our job, you can be in a show or in a TV programme one day and then cleaning your bath the next. It's strange that along the way you meet some really famous people and yet people imagine that your life is like that all the time. I have made friends with people in the business, but I have kept my friends outside as well. There's nothing like them as they will tell you if you are being a bit too big for your boots. A fan once said to my Aunty Teresa:

"Oh my word you are their aunty; do you go to their house?"

Aunty wasted no time at all in saying, "Yes, of course I do, and they come to mine."

The fan was so impressed with my aunty. She continued by saying that she thought it must be such an honour to have the Nolans coming to her house. My aunty looked on totally bemused but it was the bit that followed that made me howl with laughter.

The fan said, "Do you get your best tea set out and serve them when they come?"

Aunty, ever the practical person replied, "No! I don't. If they come to my house they can make their own tea. They can make me one as well while they're at it."

It's nice that people still recognise us though. Even if they think we don't make our own tea.

Bernie was eventually laid to rest in Blackpool. A beautiful headstone had been made which looked perfect with everyone's favourite picture of her in a permanent place. There had been a lot of legal red tape before we could do this. Bernie had wished that she be interred next to her stillborn baby, Kate, who had been buried in the same cemetery. You would think that was all perfectly straightforward, but it was far from easy. Kate had been buried in the children's section of the crematorium's graveyard and they wouldn't allow Bernie to be buried there, so a special order had to be obtained to enable the authorities to exhume baby Kate. That was a terrible, grisly ordeal for everyone concerned. As well as taking a lot of time for the paperwork to be processed, it had to go through the local authority and the coroner. Eventually, permission was given, and it was carried out in private with Bernie's ashes being buried afterwards. It really is a perfect spot. We were glad that she chose to be in Blackpool where her family are able to tend the grave. As Steve is a frequent visitor to the town it meant that he would also be able to visit her grave regularly. The whole family were able to get together and have a drink and chat about how we had been coping with our grief.

It was a sad day, but I am glad we were all together. I went home whilst Steve and Erin went back to Brian's house. We had now made up with Linda but she had become very depressed again. The death of her husband had left her totally bereft and she hadn't recovered from his death before she received the news that Bernie was terminally ill.

Chapter 11

Moving Forward

2014

After Bernie's passing we all just tried to get on with our day-to-day lives; Maureen went back on her nationwide tour of *Blood Brothers*. It's funny actually because all of my sisters have done the show expect for Coleen and me. I don't know how I'd feel about taking on the role as Mrs Johnstone as I've seen all the girls play the part. I wonder how I would play the character. When Denise played the role she performed it in a very Irish accent that the producers liked, so it would be interesting to see how I would adapt the role if it ever came knocking. Coleen went back to the second seat on the *Loose Women* panel after taking a break for a couple of years. The show was undergoing a big shake-up and they wanted to bring her back after she had decided to walk away just two years earlier.

Things were good between Coleen and me. It seemed that losing Bernie had put everything into perspective for us. I wanted my baby sister back in my life and I guess she wanted to have me back in hers.

Coleen invited Amy and me to her house. It was the first time I had been to her new home in Wilmslow, Cheshire, which she had moved into after leaving Blackpool. I was apprehensive about going, but in the end it was fine. As I pulled up outside her beautiful house, she met us at the front door with her dogs running around the car. As we walked into the front porch I was just captivated by the beauty and warmth of her home. She gave us the tour of the house while Ryder had fun on the trampoline in the garden. We sat and drank mugs of tea and it was like no time at all had passed. We never mentioned the tour or the argument, nor did the subject of she and Denise becoming friends again come up. My aunty would be turning eighty soon and that was going to be a big celebration. "Before I got in the car to head home, I asked Coleen if she would like to come to the party. She smiled and said, "of course I'd love to come".

Over the next year or so everything just ticked by, without any hiccups, thank goodness. Linda entered *Celebrity Big Brother* in the winter of 2014 and was whisked down to London on New Year's Day after ringing in the New Year the night before.

One date in the diary for that year was our Aunty Teresa's 80th birthday, we were to throw her a surprise party with all her family and friends around her. Once again, Denise took control of the party and arranged everything, with a little help from the rest of us. She organised the cake, invitation's, catering,

With the urgency that Denise put in her texts for Aunty Teresa's birthday party and the calls she made, you would have thought it was happening the following week. She had 'Save The Date' cards printed and sent out and it was planned to be a surprise. We were all to be involved and given details of what we had to do, which would be carried out with military precision. She had two bands booked, one of which were the fantastic Flip!, who I have mentioned before, and she also booked a band that could back the family. She had friends and family coming from all over the place. There was a touch of sadness as one of her cousins became seriously ill just as he was setting off for the UK. John Stanistreet had been living in Bali for several years and had decided to come over to help Aunty celebrate, but she was never to see him again. She was fond of John, so it did put a dampener on her mood. As far as Aunty was concerned, she was having a meal in a restaurant with lots of people joining her.

Denise had arranged a tiara for Aunty Teresa. She had her hair styled and wore a beautiful cobalt blue dress. All her immediate family had turned up and were hidden away inside the club awaiting her arrival. My brothers and sisters were going to be standing outside the club awaiting her arrival.

"The taxi's here, Aunty," Denise called. It always took Aunty forever to get from A to B because she needs a walking stick.

As Aunty got to the end of Denise's garden she saw she had organised a limousine for the short trip.

Quite a few got in the car with her, mainly her great nephews and nieces whom she loved to be surrounded by. She said to me as she got in, "Why has Denise gone to all this trouble? I will feel a bit of a fool arriving at a restaurant in this car."

She was even more mystified when the car pulled into the car park of the club. Denise mentioned something about picking someone up. As the car stopped, all the family came out of the door and greeted her. It was such a special moment. As she made her way into the main concert room the band struck up Stevie Wonder's 'Happy Birthday' with everyone giving her the loudest cheer as she took her seat.

Denise had pulled all the stops out making her a video that even featured her wedding day – taken on cine film. Aunty sobbed with joy and cried a few tears for her husband, Jim, who had died a few years before. We all sang a song with the band as she watched, and she was delighted. A photo was taken that included everyone who attended with her most treasured present that night was a photo taken with all her nieces and nephews surrounding her.

Coleen was now back in Aunty's life and we were all moving in the right direction. It was sad that Coleen and Denise didn't have a longer chat, but Coleen made a point of praising Denise for how well she had done in organising the party. Both had a nice moment.

Alex graduated from University in June 2014. She was pregnant again but not showing at all. Several of us attended the ceremony at the Winter Gardens. Alex got her cap and gown and we could not have been more proud. She didn't want to waste that education so quickly set about getting herself a teaching job. It had been a long-held ambition to qualify as a teacher and she had now succeeded. You could tell by the way she spoke to Vinny and offered words of encouragement when seeing he was able to solve the problem while playing with his word games. She had a few interviews at local schools and was offered a position in all but one of them. Before long she was taken on by a local Catholic school, but this was going to be a problem for her once the new baby came along as she would obviously need to be at school while someone looked after the new baby. Fortunately, by cutting my office job days down to three a week, I would in a position to have the baby.

For Maureen's sixtieth birthday that same month, she wanted a big holiday and chose Florida. Nearly all of the family went along together with a few friends. Denise and Tom didn't go because Denise doesn't like very hot weather and it was going to be very hot in Orlando in June so she declined. Maureen understood and was fine about that and said she would miss them both.

We all stayed on a fabulous complex called Orange Lake Resort and visited all the parks again, which I will never get tired of. On the night of

Maureen's birthday, we had a private room at Portafino's Hotel, about twenty minutes from where we were staying, where we had dinner. It had an Italian theme and she had two Italian men playing guitars and gorgeous Italian music just for her. The hotel had its own beach so after dinner we strolled outside and had drinks in the moonlight and again the fabulous Italian music to which we all sang along.

On the return journey to our own apartment, I drove myself Aunty, Amy, Ryder and Laura. I had lost the heel off one of my shoes, but it really didn't matter as we were only going back to our apartment. Unfortunately, after driving for about ten minutes I realised I must have taken a wrong turning and instead of going back to Orange Lake, the signs were saying we were going towards Chicago. I pulled into a lay-by where there was a shop open and got out of the car to ask directions forgetting about my broken shoe. I walked over to the entrance with a very pronounced limp, one leg being higher than the other, opened the door and limped in. There were about three or four men inside, all black and, forgetting I was in America, I stupidly asked if anyone spoke English. Needless to say, there was a short silence while they all looked at me as if I was mad. However, I think they took pity on me when I explained where I was from and that we were lost as they told me how to get back to where we needed to be. What should have been a twenty-minute drive took two hours, but we laughed so much in the car on the journey back it was worth it. The whole night was magical, even the journey home, and one I shall never forget.

That same year, Linda, Alex and I took part in *Celebrity Pressure Pad* along with two of Linda's friends Sue and Lou. John Barrowman was the host and I have always been a fan of his so was looking forward to meeting him. I was not disappointed, he was great fun, very cheeky and I loved being in his company.

The show itself went by in a flash and we found ourselves on the winning team. We raised a few quid for the charity which was the main thing. CBBC TV presenters, Sam Nixon and Mark Rhodes, were on the opposing team. They had gone quite far in the *X Factor* before branching out into comedy where they had become firm favourites on children's TV. They had also brought their families along. The show was filmed in Glasgow, and we were treated very well having plenty of laughs in the green room. Some of the questions were stinkers. I was asked what chromophobia was. In case you don't know, it's the fear of black and white!

Linda, Alex and I also took part in the Midnight Moonwalk that year to raise money for Breast Cancer Research. It was really amazing seeing thousands of women and quite a lot of men at the starting line at midnight, all in various modes of dress and all in pink.

We walked past London landmarks, several of which were lit up for our event. Many of those taking part had agreed to walk the thirteen-mile course and wore flashing light outfits and carried illuminated flags and torches. Annie, my sister-in-law, and her friends including the wonderful actress and singer Jackie Scott, managed to complete the full twenty-six miles. When I got back home, I found that two of my toes were really badly bruised and both of my big toenails eventually fell off. I had worn the comfiest of trainers for the walk but still got injured. It was worth it because it raised cash and awareness for something that has affected not just my family, but most families so much.

Alex was finally showing a bump as her pregnancy advanced, so we got into the Christmas spirit with double the excitement. Alex's due date was Christmas Day. We were all so excited that she might give birth on the actual day. Vinny, in particular, was desperate for the baby to make an appearance and when the day arrived, Alex came into Denise's house as if nothing was out of the ordinary. Vinny was beyond excited having already opened all his presents from Santa Claus at home.

On the other hand, I had turned into a mad woman. I was in the kitchen and must have been drugged or delirious when I had offered to cook for everyone. Even Brian and Annie would be joining us this year. No pressure then.

As the guests began arriving, I was knee deep in gravy, turkey and sprouts. They all bid each other 'Happy Christmas' before popping into the kitchen to extend their wishes to me. As they approached they were told, "GET OUT – GET OUT!"

I did say I loved Christmas; I didn't say I was an angel, especially with a thousand dishes that needed to come together at the same time. By the time I sat down to eat my food I had no appetite but just about managed to get some ham and turkey inside me.

Brian made a lovely speech and said, "Thank you Matron."

I was later heard saying to everybody, "I will never, ever do that again. If I suggest it at any time tell me that I am not to do it."

Everyone seemed to enjoy the food and I will never know how my mother did all of that for about twenty-five people every year in the tiniest of ovens in a kitchen that was so small. We never gave her any help with the cooking because she said she managed better left on her own. However, we did do the washing up—no dishwashers back then. I did take cooking more seriously when I got married and think it was a case of having to. Especially after I left the act for a short spell when Amy was born. I can honestly say that I eat to live, not live to eat. I love eating out or at someone's home when invited but I can't say I enjoy cooking.

After a quiet Boxing Day, when most of us met up and had a natter with turkey sandwiches and salad, we headed home for some much-needed relaxation.

Later that night, Alex began to feel as if something was happening with her baby and the following day she was admitted to hospital. I was actually in the birthing room with her and so was Steve. Everything seemed to be going along fine until the midwife said the baby wasn't turning and they would have to turn her manually. Alex and Steve were taken away to another room and I was asked to stay where I was as the doctor would now have to come to assist the midwife. I think I was only in that room for about twenty minutes, but it felt like twenty hours. Eventually a nurse came and asked me if I was OK which immediately set me off crying. I was so worried about my little girl, her baby and husband. Not knowing what was happening was terrible. She gave me a hug and told me everything was going to be OK, which it was. In about another ten minutes Steve came in with the nurse pushing the bed with Alex still on it but this time holding a beautiful baby girl. It had been a difficult birth, but everything turned out perfectly. The baby was to be called Nevaeh Gabrielle. Nevaeh is heaven spelt backwards and I fell in love with the second I saw her.

Nevaeh

She was so perfect; blond, petite and with the widest eyes I have ever seen on a baby since Vinny. Alex was content but exhausted.

Alex, Steve and Vinny had stayed with me and Auntie during Alex's pregnancy, as they had decided to buy a bigger house now the family was extending and Steve hit on the idea that he would take a job on the oil rigs on the Irish Sea, which entailed long hours and days at a time, but the salary was insane. As a qualified electrician he could earn fabulous wages. He took his exams and tried it for a couple of contracts, but he couldn't bear to be away from his home and family. He earned good money anyhow so they could enjoy a comfortable life.

Before she got pregnant Alex had taken on a job as a teaching assistant and really loved working with the primary school kids. Her first job had been working alongside me in the insolvency service, but she never went back after Vinny came along. She was now focused on getting her qualifications up to a required level where she could become a qualified teacher. Alex is academically bright and I had the feeling she had what it took to knuckle down and get what was needed. We had never had anyone in our family who had gone to university before and the things she had to learn left me speechless. I never understood where she got the energy to be a housewife, mother, stepmother and hold down a job all at the same time. The route she took involved a lot of on-the-job training which would only hold her in good stead. Although it looked like being a long job, I was thrilled for her.

They stayed with me until Nevaeh was about 9 months old and their new house was ready for them to move into. I absolutely loved that time as it gave me an opportunity to make a fuss of all of them. I may have spent my life in public as part of a sister act but behind closed doors, I was truly at my happiest when I had my family with me. When I was away in Panto or Summer Season it was always the hardest thing to leave my girls. When they were babies, I could take them with me, even when they were on school holidays. We are so close that never a day goes by when I don't speak to them or see them. I cried on the first night on my own after Alex, Steve, Vinny and baby Nevaeh left.

When I visited the house after it was completed and they had moved in, I thought it was absolutely gorgeous and couldn't believe all the changes they had made. They were so thrilled to be starting together as a family of their own. I love Steve and I know he loves Alex unconditionally. He had a son, called Danny, from a previous relationship (so many Danny's and Tommy's in our family!). Everyone in our family loves Danny and he spends a lot of his time with Alex and his dad. Steve is a fabulous father. When I see how dads are nowadays, compared to how they were not so many years ago I am so impressed. Dads are far more demonstrative with their love and affection. Steve always has time to spend with his children and his love is evident to all who see him with them.

Alex had the normal amount of time off work for maternity leave and when she started back at work, I was happy to look after Nevaeh as well as Ryder. Ryder was due to start school soon so I believed I could manage. It was a disappointment that Ryder didn't get into the same school as Vinny, but he started attending another local Catholic school. It did mean that I would have a lot of school runs to do. On Monday morning I would go to Alex's house and pick up Vinny and Nevaeh, drop Vinny at school, then go back and pick Amy up and take her to work. She had recently moved into her own home quite nearby. I would then take Ryder and Nevaeh back to my home. It may sound like a lot to do but any grandmother will tell you that it's not a chore, it's a joy, particularly for me. You want to do whatever you can for your children, and I am no exception.

****

2015

I would be sixty-five that year and had already decided to cut my working hours down to three days a week. It seemed practical from a babysitting point of view and it made sense because I wasn't as young as I used to be. The other side of me loved my job though. There would be no point in retiring as I had made some really good friends at work and always enjoyed going in. Some people hate their job but I never felt that way. My showbiz career was now firmly on my terms and if I wanted to do something I would do it, if not then that was also my decision.

A Blackpool musician called Stephen Pierre had asked me to appear in a show at Blackpool Tower where I would sing with a full orchestra. It was only a twenty-minute set but I agreed to take part in the show and was so glad I did as it was the first chance I had of singing with an orchestra on my own. It was held in the main ballroom and I wore a beautiful, full length, red evening gown covered in sequins. As I performed, some of the audience got up to dance a waltz while I sang. It was infectious and I came off the stage on a high.

Early in the year I was invited to Coleen's 50th birthday party which she was holding at the Radisson Hotel at Manchester Airport. I enjoyed the evening. It was great fun and lovely to see lots of family and friends I hadn't seen in a long time. I shared my room with a good family friend, Celia, who came back to Blackpool for a few days afterwards.

The whole year was a relatively calm one for our family. Linda had gone to Ireland to work in the musical *Menopause The Musical.* It was a new role for her and she seemed to be enjoying it.

Maureen was away touring with *Blood Brothers* before landing a part in a major production of *Footloose* which would tour all the major theatres in the UK.

I was able to concentrate my time with the rest of my family and to consolidate my own thoughts on my life. I had already been involved with several charities and wanted to give more of my time to two in particular: Alzheimer's and Breast Cancer Care. The people at Alzheimer's were fantastic and asked me to all sorts of events and make short speeches. I had not been used to making serious points before. It's one thing being asked to introduce a song or my sisters when we were on stage, but this was totally new. I made sure I did some research and spent a long time learning to craft words that would have an impact. I wanted people to listen to what I had to say about my own experience and to be inspired to act on them. It was a totally nerve-wracking experience but, after I did it each time, I came away thinking it meant something. I took part in events on radio and in person around the Fylde coast. Many of them appeared in the local press which gave the story more of a punch. I even went to our local hospital and gave a speech to staff and visitors.

I recorded my little single, 'Christmas Time Is Here' and went on the promotional trail. I knew it wouldn't set the charts on fire as it had such a lot to compete with. I did read in *NME* magazine (in hysterics) that Justin Bieber had selected it as his favourite new Christmas song and the one he thought would be the most successful of the crop that year. It was great fun promoting it which I summed up at the time as a nice little Christmas ditty. I still think it is to be fair and it's still available on iTunes.

One of the nicest things I get to do at Christmas is a visit to the Clifton Hospital in Blackpool. I had been asked to become a patron of the Just Good Friends charity in Blackpool, run by a fabulous lady called Bev Sykes, which I was delighted to accept. For the fourth year in a row, I went along with a friend called James, who is involved with the charity, and had dressed as Santa Claus. As well as the two of us, there were loads of other helpers from the charity as well as police officers, community support workers and the fire service. All year they raise money to buy presents and then visit the elderly at hospital to hand them out. Not everyone has friends and family to give them gifts, so taking part is a really magical experience. The gifts aren't Armani handbags and Chanel perfume, but you can tell they are appreciated by the look on the recipient's face. The nurses had decorated the ward with a tree covered in tinsel and if anything is going to get you in the Christmas spirit, that will.

Chapter 12

I'm Having a Party and You're All Invited

2017

At the beginning of the year I decided to host a charity ball. It would be to raise funds for the Alzheimer's Society. I had been to many charity balls and thought, how hard could it be to organise? Especially with our profile.

I spoke to the Alzheimer Society and they said someone would come to our first committee meeting. That was the first thing I was unaware of. They recommend that you have a proper committee, with a secretary, treasurer and chairman. We used Denise's house for the first meeting, and I appointed Jacqui as treasurer. She is known to be careful with money so I knew it would be in safe hands with her. Denise was on the committee too along with my friend Linda and Amy's friends Laura and Leah. A local councillor called Peter, who did a lot of work for The Alzheimer Society, also joined us.

We would have lots of meeting over the next few weeks and months. It was at this time it began to sink in that there was a lot more to hosting a ball than just booking it and hoping everyone would pay and turn up with full pockets. We had a break-even point to reach to get in sufficient funds to pay for room hire, food and entertainment. If I didn't make that then there would be little point in going ahead. I also had to provide a deposit of a thousand pounds to secure the venue on the date we had in mind. My Aunty Teresa generously offered to give me the deposit and said she wanted no repayment as she wanted to donate it to the charity.

I also wanted a couple of guest speakers who would chat for a while, but not hopefully lecture people into falling asleep. I arranged for my brother, Brian, to compere the show with help from a DJ, who is also a drag queen called Chris D'Bray. I thought that might be a bit different. I had booked Flip! as the live entertainment and our friend, Adam, who often DJs for us, would provide the late-night music.

Then I had the task of contacting local and national companies to ask for raffle and auction prizes. It was horrific! I had no idea how hard it would be. I now appreciate that some of these companies must have hundreds of similar requests all the time.

I had a letter drawn up with The Alzheimer Society's registered charity number on it together with all the information needed to explain what I was asking for. It included who I was and my connection with the Society and how my mum had died from this most horrible disease. I sent it to every company and individual I could think of. The result was disheartening. On so many occasions I received a reply saying:

'Dear Ms. Nolan,

Thank you for your email. You may be aware that we receive literally hundreds of requests like yours each year. We have, sadly, reached our limit on the amount of prizes we are able to donate to charity this year but you could try again next year. Good luck with your event and your fund-raising endeavours.

Yours Sincerely…'

I think that for every twenty emails I sent out, just one was successful. So many times they didn't even reply. I do see it from their point of view. When the Nolans were at the peak of their success, we had hundreds of such requests by letter and phone and we felt awful having to turn so many down. It's so difficult trying to be a success and make money and at the same time wanting to help other people who aren't so successful and have no money. That was the position I found myself in and it caused me a lot of sleepless nights. This time, I tried everything from airlines to football clubs, hotels to train companies.

By the time the ball arrived though I had made a breakthrough and all my hard work finally paid off. I had a table full of donated prizes for a raffle and whole raft of auction items. Denise got me tickets to see *The Elvis Show* that was touring at the time. Coleen arranged two prizes. One was train tickets to London with Virgin Trains to see *Loose Women* and meet the panel after the show. Another were tickets for a show and to meet and greet superstar girl band, Little Mix.

I also got twelve vouchers for different local restaurants.

Anyone who knows Linda will know that she is Osmond mad! Don't ask me how but she was able to get Jimmy Osmond to send tickets for his show along with signed photos and CDs. I had a signed photo of the Arsenal Football Club team, the only football club to send anything, although all the others I had emailed did send a nice reply.

There were prizes from local jewellers and a hairdresser and spas and theatre tickets for shows at our local theatres including The Opera House and the Grand, etc. I also received some wonderful prizes from a friend called Liz Emmett, who had organised a few charity balls herself for breast cancer in memory of Bernie. She gave me a fabulous prize of a holiday at a four-star hotel with an all-inclusive package complete with flights and transfers – for four people! That was a great prize, along with some other great prizes and lots of advice. I was sure the items would raise a lot of money. I even went to the local press in January to start begging for coverage of the ball I had arranged for October. Local radio station Radio Lancashire also helped out with publicity. I needed close to two hundred to attend to make a decent profit.

Our committee sourced various locations for the event, and we arranged for one of the best hotels in Blackpool to provide hosting facilities. The ball seemed to be taking such a lot of my time and energy, but it was worth it. I was looking forward to opening the Blackpool event of International Women's Day at the Winter Gardens in March. It was a great day and I enjoyed making my speech and meeting old and new faces at the ever-growing event.

In between working at my day job I also took part in Dementia Awareness Week, which was another round of speeches and appearances, doing my bit to try to get people to take notice and to join in. It also gave me a chance to let people know about my upcoming ball in October. We finally hit the break-even point for the ball and the money started coming in. As the function drew nearer, the gifts and prizes came in thick and fast and I knew they would get people's hands in their pockets. The hotel had decorated the room beautifully and on the day of the event my nerves really began to kick in.

My friend Jacqui and I had a room booked so we could get changed and chill out once the function room was finished. Of course, everyone and Uncle Tom Cobley came in to have their hair done and apply make-up. It was a really great atmosphere. All my sisters had bought tickets and, yet again, my family and a few friends from Ireland didn't fail me and arrived from Ireland to get the party going!

I had done a seating plan that, hopefully, would suit everyone. Denise would be at the same table as our cousins Angie and Val, Coleen's son, Jake, his friend and also our friends, Adam, Carl and Lee.

Coleen was joined by Maureen, Brian, Annie and friends on another table and Linda had a table with her friend Sue, Kim, Liz and *X Factor* legend, Mary Byrne.

The Hetheringtons had come along en-masse with all of their friends and families. I opened the evening by talking a little about my mum, as the evening was in her memory, and a professor from Lancaster University gave a short talk on Alzheimer's. Not meaning to boast, but the evening was a total success. We raised over seven thousand pounds, and it was all due to the amazing hard work of my committee and the generosity of so many people. As the night drew to a close people were saying they had all had the best night for ages. They all wanted to put their names down for next year's event. I had to have a long, hard think about whether I could put my friends through all that again. I swore that I wouldn't, but soon afterwards I started to think aloud to people, saying, "For next year's ball, I think I will have it where the entertainment is..."

Just before Christmas, Linda was heading into rehearsals in Preston for her forthcoming panto in the Guildhall. All the grandkids love panto and were looking forward to seeing their aunty Linda playing the good fairy in *Jack and the Beanstalk*. As Linda doesn't drive, she was delighted it was being staged so nearby at Preston. She would be able to commute on the train and, on some days, could get friends and family to take her and bring her back.

Pantomime today is not the same as it used to be with performance times and the length of the run. Back in the day they would last almost three months and performances would usually be in the evening with a couple of matinee shows. Now the trend is for morning shows and evenings have become the late performances. During the run, which usually lasts about three weeks, there are perhaps only two shows a week that have the curtain up at seven thirty p.m. Despite the ordeal of having to get up early (which none of my family is keen on), Linda was happy to be back on stage.

On one particular day she got to Preston train station and fell down the stairs that lead to the platforms. It was quite a fall, and she injured her leg and ankle. For that day at least she was out of the show. A visit to the hospital saw that she had not broken any bones so that was good, but she was very badly bruised. If it weren't for the fact she was wearing ankle boots they thought she would have certainly fractured her ankle. Our family have always called her 'Lucky Linda' for if there is anyone who will trip or fall it will be her. On reflection, she had suffered quite a few tumbles and we wondered if she had arthritis or something similar that made her legs weak on stairs. She was able to resume rehearsals shortly after and went on to have a successful run in the production.

Shortly after Linda's panto had finished she found she had been successful in getting a part in a new musical featuring the music of Madness called *Our House.* She was delighted!

Fast forward a couple of months: it was a Saturday evening and I was snuggling on the sofa watching TV when my phone lit up. It was Denise and when I picked up I could hear her on the other end of the line sounding very panicked. I couldn't make out what she was saying so asked her to slow down and repeat it.

She said, "You'll have to come round; Linda has had an accident. I'm with her now and she is in agony."

Denise wailed down the phone. She is terrible when she sees anyone in pain and just can't bear it. She has fainted more than once at seeing someone in pain. I jumped up and ran upstairs franticly getting dressed and grabbed my car keys that were sitting on the sideboard, snatched my jacket off the hooks beside the front door and made a beeline towards my car. When I pulled up outside Linda's, I could see that all the lights downstairs were turned on. I saw Roma, Maureen's youngest granddaughter, looking out of the window and then she darted off to tell the others of my arrival. When I walked in, I could see Linda on the ground at the top of the stairs in a heap and crying in agony.

It transpired that she had been babysitting and had gone upstairs for something and tripped, or her leg gave way near the top, and she landed quite awkwardly. She said that she heard a distinct crack as she hit the floor. She called down to Maureen's granddaughter, Ava, to tell her she'd had an accident and to fetch her mobile. Also staying at Linda's was Ava's sister, Sienna, who was distressed at seeing her aunty in pain. Apparently, they were also upset that the planned sleepover wasn't going to happen!

Denise called the ambulance whilst I did my best to reassure the kids that everything would be OK. As it was a Saturday night, the ambulance service was rushed off its feet with all the revellers having accidents, fights and whatever else especially in Blackpool. They told Denise that the ambulance would not be able to get to Linda until midnight.

I told the girls to sit in the lounge saying we would get it sorted and picked up the phone and called the ambulance back. I wasn't stroppy or rude, but said, "My sister has had an accident. She is standing on the landing and has been there for almost an hour. She can't sit, walk, or go to the toilet and needs an ambulance now."

After a few questions, the woman on the other end of the line said, "It will be with you in twenty minutes."

Sure enough, it did arrive, even quicker than that, I think. The paramedics were amazing, as they always are. They were able to use their skills and painkillers to get Linda onto a stretcher and into the ambulance. Denise would stay with the kids, and I would go with Linda to the hospital.

I don't want to sound unkind about people, but Saturday night in the accident and emergency department at a hospital is not for the faint-hearted. As well as all the normal heartbreaking tragedies and accidents, sitting there waiting to be seen, just as many people, if not more, were arriving drunk or drugged up waiting to be seen. I am sure they are in pain, and that they must also be seen, but so often their pain is a result of their own crazy antics.

That particular night, it was bedlam. Men and women were being very loud and causing a disturbance, which the poor injured people and their relatives had to witness. As we were admitted, we were told we were looking at four hours before the doctors would see us.

As the unit was so busy Linda was wheeled on a trolley and put in a corridor. A nurse came along and took pity on Linda—I think she may have recognised us? She was so lovely and said she would put us in a side room. We didn't expect any preferential treatment and didn't want to jump any queues, but that piece of kindness really was welcomed. After all the usual chats with the medics, Linda was x-rayed and told she had a small fracture to her hip. The doctor said that she would probably need a hip replacement. We actually laughed at this. You know you are getting on a bit when your younger sister breaks a hip and needs a new one.

They couldn't do it immediately, so they were going to admit Linda to the ward and make sure she was comfortable and rested before having surgery which would probably be on the Monday. One of the first things Linda commented on was that she hoped she would be fully recovered in time for the start of her new musical. They moved her into a room where she was able to relax on her own over the weekend. The staff did everything they could to make her free of pain and reassured her that the operation was straightforward and would be successful. On the Monday, one of the doctors said that in view of her history they were going to carry out a few more scans and tests before they went ahead with the operation. She kept us informed by text; at this stage we had absolutely no indication that anything was of concern.

The scan came back, and doctors were concerned about a small area in her hip so they wanted to carry out a biopsy to be sure. The person best suited to this only came to Blackpool on certain days and to get him to carry out the procedure would mean that she would have to be transferred to Oswestry in Shropshire. Linda went by ambulance to the Midlands, and Denise as always leapt into action and rented a cottage within a short ride from the hospital.

She and Tom followed the ambulance and settled themselves into their temporary home, making sure Linda had everything she needed. Understandably, Linda was anxious but she remained upbeat. After a couple of days, Tom had to return to London for work, leaving Denise to make all the hospital visits and keep us all up to speed. She started a WhatsApp group so we could ask questions without troubling

Linda and making her go through the same story again and again.

The procedure itself was painless, and she began to take small steps with crutches. Shortly afterwards she was given the knockout blow that the growth in her hip was cancer. It was malignant and most crushing of all, it was incurable. The doctors told her what to expect and how they would treat her. When they said that it was incurable, but treatable Linda answered with, "You said that to my sister." Each time they mentioned something about new drugs and trials coming out all the time, she reiterated, "You said that to my sister." The response was the same when they told her that whilst it wasn't curable, it was treatable, and that people on their books had been living with what Linda had for fifteen years. She wasn't offhand with the medics, it was just her gallows humour, which she found a great way of coping. Linda's breast cancer had returned – in her hip. She was allowed back to Blackpool, where she was given a room of her own so she could rest properly and see visitors.

Denise's chap, Tom, would be seventy in March and Denise had decided to throw a big party for him at our local golf club. She had arranged for the members of a band Tom plays in to come up north and do a spot. We always tried to book his band to play as it gave us all the chance to sing. Lots of Tom's family are singers too, so we were all really looking forward to it. Unfortunately, Linda would not be able to make it and was gutted. A couple of her friends went to the hospital that night though and the nurses allowed them to have a mini party. She even had a couple of glasses of prosecco.

Meanwhile, we had a great time at Tom's party. Denise had flown her stepson, Tom Jnr, over from America as a surprise. Tom was so emotional when his son walked in, holding his birthday cake.

Another highlight of that night was the surprise item that Vinny and I had planned. We had rehearsed Sinatra's 'They Can't Take That Away from Me' over the last few days. Vinny didn't display any real nerves, which was amazing as he had learned the song by listening to a CD of the instrumental version but on the night, he would be singing it with me and a live band. I know it sounds big-headed, but Vinny did not sing a note out of tune. He absolutely brought the room down with everyone standing up, applauding and cheering. He took it all in his stride, smiling and bowing. I am convinced that show business will feature in his life somewhere, although he wants to be an actuary as he is incredibly intelligent. Sometimes, the draw of the stage is too strong though, especially if it is in your DNA.

Before the party Denise reached out to Coleen and asked her along to the party as we were all going to be there. Tom had been in Coleen's life since she was a kid and, to our delight, Coleen agreed and came. By now her marriage to Ray wasn't in the best shape, so it was nice to have her with us to celebrate Tom's big night. Just like that, the ill feeling that had been around since the initial disagreement in Coleen's lounge, the family feud as it was known, was over.

By April, Linda had been discharged from hospital. They had given her a cocktail of drugs and radiotherapy. She didn't have to undergo any chemotherapy this time as they had decided it would be ineffective. She decided to stay at Denise's house as she is great at looking after anyone who is ill. She will cook, clean and invest all her time in making the person feel they are safe. Most importantly, Linda would not be alone. Cancer can be a very lonely illness and being alone in bed at night can be frightening.

Linda would lean on Denise a great deal over the following months, which, I think, is how Denise likes it to be. In our whole family, Denise has always been the one to put the family first. In some ways she missed out on having friends for many years because of it.

Linda chose *Loose Women* and the *Daily Mirror* as the platforms she wanted to tell the world about her diagnosis and would be doing an interview with Coleen live from Denise's house.

On a positive note, the people at the hospital did say that they were confident they could treat Linda's cancer with injections to strengthen the bone with calcium and, at the time of writing, it has proved to be effective. The calcium has surrounded the tumour and is seemingly keeping it from spreading. It has also helped make her bones stronger.

She has never been one for doing nothing and did overdo it quite a lot. *Loose Women* wanted her to make a video diary which they would film from Denise's house again. I can understand why she agreed to such a high degree of intrusion in her life as she had been forced to withdraw from her role in the Madness musical and would need an income.

It's always a peril in show business. You can land a major role and think that you will be earning good money, only to have it taken away in a heartbeat. All my sisters and I have then been let down at the last minute in this way and there is no compensation for the lost earnings. You might even have rejected work because of something else you have signed up for but it's no use trying to sue them. If they haven't the cash for the show, they won't have cash to pay in a legal battle. On the flip side, if you are the one who walks away from a show, you can get sued. Bernie had been worried about that happening when she left *Chicago* and then her panto that year. It would be unspeakable if a company were to do that, but I know it has happened in this business of ours.

Linda also agreed to take part in a show called *In Therapy* which, as the name implies, was to cover her own battle with mental health. That programme was also mainly filmed at Denise's house.

During 2017 – 2018, I was offered a panto in the Northwest in two theatres. The schedule wasn't gruelling, and I could fit it in without too much of a struggle with my office job. The company was fairly small with a cast of young people, who I was sure would never have heard of me. I agreed to take part but, the second I put the phone down, I began to regret saying yes. My kids and my friends were all telling me that it was about time I got back on stage but I think it was just a case of nerves and my confidence being knocked.

Whenever my friends had charity events they organised, they asked me to act as compere and to sing a few songs. On each occasion, no sooner had I agreed than I felt regret. Then, once I got on stage, I felt completely at home and people told me my singing voice was holding up fine.

Soon it was time for the annual Bernie Nolan Celebration Ball. This was to become a highlight in the family calendar as we would all put our glad rags on and spend the weekend celebrating my little sister. It was a weekend affair organised by Liz Emmett, a lady who Maureen and I had met years ago when we did a gig at her hotel. Linda got to know her after she was in the Big Brother house and she would hire Linda to host concerts and later her other events ranging from New Year's Eve to Halloween Balls.

At the end of 2017, we checked into The Woburn Hotel on the Friday and arrived the night before the party. Liz had flown over two cast members from *The Waltons*! Yes, *The Waltons*, Mary McDonald who played Erin Walton and her on-screen mother Olivia Walton, played by Michael Learned. It was a very nostalgic evening as we grew up watching them on TV and here they were, honouring our little sister for the evening. We danced the night away and had a 'hooley' as we Irish say!

The next morning, we were meant to be filming for *Loose Women*. However, the night before, I had gone a little too hard on the vino and phoned the girls to tell them that I was not in a fit state to film. I felt much better after having something to eat and got into my glad rags and got the party bus over to Towcester Racecourse for the ball. The night was a spectacular event: Steve and Erin got up and said a few words. Erin had recently turned eighteen so we brought out a cake and all her aunties sang 'Happy Birthday' except for Denise, who wasn't able to attend. This was a hard moment for us all as it was Bernie's goal to be here for the milestone. Mary Byrne again was at hand to enchant us with her fabulous voice, Stavros Flatley from BGT was performing as well and Coleen's son, Shane, got the party going with his band. We had a great night from start to finish. Although, while I was there, I had a big secret that I was not allowed to share with my family, in fear it would make news.

Chapter 13

The Rover Returns?

As I walked on the cobbled stones to make my way up the set of one of the most famous streets in the country, I had to pinch myself. Here I was, auditioning for a potential role in *Coronation Street.* Who'd have thought that at my age, I would be having a shot at trying for one of the most recognisable TV shows in the world!

I was standing outside The Rovers Return clenching onto the brass handles of the famous pub, posing for a photo. I felt like a schoolgirl on a school trip. There is something about a TV studio that enchants me. Perhaps it stems from my childhood, watching all those black-and-white films and wondering how they did it. I was like a kid in a candy shop, although I wanted to play it cool hoping they wouldn't catch on.

I was sworn to absolute secrecy and agreed it was the best policy because I didn't want to risk anyone taking this opportunity away from me. I made my way to the studios in Salford Quays near Manchester early that day to do the reading; I was beyond sick with nerves. They had given me a script that featured a former character, Aunty Pam. She was the wheeler dealer who lived with Tyrone and his girlfriend at the time. One of the Corrie production team would feed me the lines and I would act them out whilst being filmed. As I waited in a green room one of the regular cast, Connor McIntyre, who played supreme baddie, Pat Phelan, walked past me. He stopped in his tracks and said in the friendliest voice, "Hello Anne, how are you, my love?"

I got up and stammered something about me thinking he was incredible playing his character. It wasn't fawning flattery; I am a massive Corrie fan and I did think he was fabulous. The fact that he knew who I was made my day. He gave me a hug and asked how we were coping since Bernie had passed away. He seemed to know all about our careers, which was such a thrill.

There wasn't a specific part that I was going for. It was just a screen test to see if I could act and that they might want to use me at some point. Provided I was any good, that is. I told Pat that I hoped if I did succeed, I would get to work with him.

The scene itself went fine. I had rehearsed the couple of pages so many times that I knew the parts of everyone who spoke in the scene, so I didn't have to refer to the script at all. I asked them if they wanted me to speak in an English accent or an Irish one and they said I could choose whichever I wanted. So, I stuck with an Irish accent. Afterwards we had a coffee and I was told that I had done very well. They were pleased with my delivery and timing. They told me that there weren't any specific parts being cast just then but that they would certainly put me in the approved candidate's section and if any part came up, which they thought appropriate in the future, they would use me.

I left the studio elated. I still don't know if they say that to everyone who has a screen test with them, and I don't want to know. The main thing was that I had got as far as screen testing. I would be in my element if I was ever to land a role in Corrie. It was not easy keeping the screen test quiet, but I did manage it for a few weeks until, one Sunday, I read in newspapers that I had done the screen test and that I hoped to be a Corrie star.

When Coleen agreed to take part in an *All Stars' Celebrity Big Brother* earlier in the year, which she eventually won, she disclosed that she and Ray had not been getting along. I had heard on the grapevine that things were not going well for quite some time and when Coleen left the CBB House, they were supposed to spend time together and sort out their differences. They limped on for a while before they decided to call it a day. I was upset for Coleen. When all is said and done, she loved him; in fact, she was nuts about him. It was revealed by Coleen that Ray had said he didn't find her attractive anymore but said he was still in love with her. She must have been devastated to have revealed all this to camera on the show *In Therapy*.

I felt sorry for Coleen; this was her second marriage to fail. She had fallen in love many times and always invested so much effort into relationships but, more often than not, they had let her down.

Maureen has become quite an accomplished musical theatre actress and I was genuinely pleased that she was having a good time on the tour and getting good reviews. As we trooped to the stage door a few people stopped us for photographs and autographs which was lovely.

Maureen was going to be back in the Opera House at Blackpool for a Christmas show which would be good as we would see more of her over the holidays. She had been very unhappy whilst touring a couple of years beforehand after finding out her own marriage had broken down. Her husband, Richie, was a lovely guy and we all had a lot of time for him so it would be strange not having him part of our lives.

Anyway, Richie and Maureen were going to split, and I was sad for them. They had been together more than twenty years but married for only a few of them. Maureen seemed to be handling things quite well, superficially at least. She decided she didn't want to stay full time in the marital home and chose to spend time at Denise's house or at the house I share with my aunty. It would take some adjusting to, but she needed to be around us. I know that Maureen had been devastated about us all falling out as we had worked together, even after Bernie and Coleen had left the act.

By the time she returned to Blackpool for the Christmas show, she was more of less living out of a suitcase. On some of the days she was staying with Denise and other times she was at my aunty's house. My aunty never questioned her when she stayed over. I had recently finished renovating one of the spare bedrooms and Maureen put her stuff in there.

Chapter 14

Topping the Bill

2019

It was now over ten years since the release of my first book, *Anne's Song.* The only time I saw the book was when I was dusting down the cabinet in my lounge at home, where I have a copy, or after a show when a fan would appear and ask me to sign a copy. I was happy with the book but had moved on, working on other projects and at my office job. I was now able to work three days a week on a part-time contract, which allowed me to spend more time with the grandkids! I got a phone call on one of my days off from my manager, Marc; he had someone he was in communications with about a new project.

Apparently, there was a group of people who were interested in making a musical based on my book. My initial reaction was to laugh. Considering the delicate nature of some of the contents of my first book I couldn't imagine what kind of songs they would write to cover such topics. Would anyone want to hear a song about child abuse? Marc debated the point saying that *Evita* was hardly a barrel of laughs or *Blood Brothers* for that matter.

The nature of the musical was that it wasn't going to be a Nolans' jukebox. The story would be a biographical account of my life and the songs featured would be brand new songs. As most of my life had been amazing, I began to see merit in the idea.

Marc had been working closely with Adam Morley who was an award-winning theatre director and producer. I had heard of him in recent times, and I must confess it certainly made me sit upright and listen closer. The script had already been started. Paul Wood had made a rough copy and was keen to have me work with him to supervise and make a creative input into the final product.

The Nolans had a songwriter back in the day called Terry Bradford. He is the man who wrote our first Epic Records release, 'Harry My Honolulu Lover'. The song had been intended to represent the UK in the 1979 Eurovision Song Contest and we had been robbed of a chance to perform the song that we had rehearsed to perfection live. Apparently, there had been a big fuss at the BBC after two technicians had been involved in a punch-up over something or other. The Trades Unions had got involved after one of the men was dismissed and when the BBC refused to reinstate him, they went on strike – right at the time we were sitting in the dressing room at the Royal Albert Hall. When the BBC pulled the plug, we were sent home, gutted and the press called us 'sore losers' which stung. The juries around the country were forced to listen to a tape recording but missed out on the chance to see our performance.

Terry, it seemed, was also on board with the project. He would be tasked with writing twenty-three new songs. The score also featured up-tempo tunes with funny lyrics and foot-tapping, feel-good songs. The show was workshopped by the University of London a couple of years ago and then the pandemic threw a spanner in the works for the production.

Meanwhile I was booked to do panto but this time in summer? Yes I know, it was July 2018 and there was a heatwave outside and I found myself performing inside the Albert Halls in Bolton. It was the first time I worked with this production company and the man behind it all was a young guy called Jo Purdy. I thought he was very brave to take on this task as this was not a tiny theatre and if he could pull this off, then he deserved my attention and support.

I was offered the leading role and he had chosen some beautiful costumes for the cast. Jo turned out to be a lovely man. There was nothing he wouldn't do to make the show happen and was prepared to sell tickets, appear in the show and clean the toilets if he had to. We had a short rehearsal time and the cast were divine! I know it's easy to say that as performers are expected to big up the cast when they are interviewed, but it's not always harmony. For the summer panto I sang 'Climb Every Mountain' from *The Sound Of Music* and 'Somewhere' from *West Side Story*, which are quite challenging vocally. Fortunately, the show generated enough interest to make it onto ITV news and we did good business for the run.

Linda carried on with her treatment. By now she had been staying at Denise's house for more than a year. She was unable to carry out stage work, so she would rely on work from TV and interviews.

We were all gathered in one of Blackpool's top venues, 'Viva', in the heart of the town centre, to celebrate Linda's 60th birthday. We had a fantastic party, complete with a live orchestra, catering, beautiful flower arrangements and with all her family and friends there, having travelled from near and far.

Her friend Liz Emmett had organised the party without letting her know what was in store for her. The highlight of the night was to be Liz surprising Linda by sending her and her friend, Sue, together with our sister Maureen to Las Vegas for a week. Sue had also become a great friend to all of us and the trip's expenses were to be all covered. For Linda, there was increased delight when she was told they would be going to see Donny & Marie Osmond at their Las Vegas residency. During the party Linda had asked us all to sing as a family so we all got together and sang Barbra Streisand's 'The Way We Were'. Afterwards, when we finished, the whole room erupted.

Normal life continued that year. A typical day for me would be getting up and going to work at my job in the office as a civil servant and, on my days off, I'd look after my gorgeous granddaughter Nevaeh. During the summer we'd take days out to Lytham and meet with some of my sisters or my friend Jaquie who would bring her grandson along who was of a similar age to Nevaeh. More often we'd go around to Jaquie's as she has a beautiful home with a gigantic garden at the back where we could watch the kids play and catch up over a cup of tea whilst basking under the lovely sunshine.

It was around this time that there were talks about a big Nolans' project that was being worked on. It had come at the time Linda and Maureen had started working with a young chap called Dermot McNamara. He had established his own talent agency and had achieved a lot in his very early career. I hadn't met him at the time but had heard of great things he was doing for the girls. I didn't pay much attention to this as, over the years, you would hear on a regular basis that someone was going to put us back on the road or finance an album, and then nothing would come of it.

It wasn't until one day that in our siblings' WhatsApp chat that Linda wrote in and asked if we would be willing to go and speak to the powers that be about a TV show giving the viewers a look into the life of our family. We met with the production company who later dispatched a film crew to follow us on a day-to-day basis for a week. With the recorded material, they had shot a pilot and brought it to the network Quest Red. It was decided that the channel wanted to do a travel show with us and came up with the title *In The Mood For Cruising* before being changed to *The Nolans Go Cruising*. The show was given the green light with filming to commence in February 2020 to help celebrate the 40th anniversary of 'I'm in The Mood for Dancing'.

Chapter 15

Making Waves

I was topping the bill in Bolton's Christmas pantomime, Cinderella, in 2019. Anyone who knows me will know how much I love Christmas. I am famous for my Christmas tree and take pride in decorating the house with decorations I have collected over the years. It was a nice treat though being able to work so close to home. I have had pantomime seasons all over England where I'd have to drive hours to get back home, so it was real luxury to be able to make the short commute from Blackpool to Bolton.

Panto can often be hard work; although, from an audience's perspective, they often think it must be great fun which doesn't require much work. However, you often have two performances a day, one in the morning and another in the evening. Nowadays, sometimes you can be delt with a three-show day, which is hard work requiring a lot of energy and stamina to stick to the schedule. It was so lovely to have my daughters bring their kids along so they could see me up there making their Christmas even more magical.

We had a quiet New Year in our house as 2020 was gearing up to be a very busy year with my diary filling up. Before I knew it, towards the end of January the preparations for *The Nolans Go Cruising* had commenced.

A week later we got together for a special evening in Lytham, when we all had a night out supporting Denise in her *Music of Judy Garland* UK tour. This was a big night for Denise as it was the first time she had taken her show back on the road for quite a while. She blew us all away with her performance on the night. I joined Denise to perform the same Judy Garland and Barbara Streisand duet of 'Get Happy/Happy Days Are Here Again' that we had sung at her 60th birthday party. I love singing that with Denise, and the audience loved it. We all had a drink in the bar after the show, which was to be one of our last get-togethers before jetting off to start filming.

I closed my eyes and clutched the arm rest as the aeroplane sprinted down the runway at Manchester Airport. We were on our way to Genoa, a coastal city at the top of Italy, where we would be meeting the cruise ship the following day. We started filming earlier in the day and we were put in a beautiful hotel in the city centre beside the port. When I checked into my room, I immediately went to look out of the window at the lovely views of the Italian streets below.

The production team had reserved a room in a fish restaurant that night where we sat around the table talking about the cruise, what it would be like and which cities we could look forward to visiting. I expressed my concerns to the girls about learning the choreography for 'I'm In The Mood For Dancing', which we were asked to sing in front of fellow passengers onboard the ship to celebrate 40 years of our hit. They reassured me it would be fine, and they'd help me along with it.

When we pulled up in front of MSC *Grandiosa*, we were all dumbfounded, the sheer size of this ship had all of us left without words. It was a beautiful, luxurious ship which had only been launched a month before, so we were one of its early passengers.

Coleen, Linda, Maureen and me before boarding MS Grandiosa,

We checked into the ship and were escorted to our rooms by a lovely stewardess. Those of you who saw the show will remember the beautiful diamond stars, which were encased in glass down the steps and were Swarovski crystals – amazing!

Initially, I was in two minds about going before I left for the cruise. Yes, we had all made up since the reunion tour, but I did have a feeling that this could either be an amazing experience or it could go terribly wrong.

Joining me on the cruise were Maureen, Linda and Coleen. Due to Denise's touring schedule, she was unable to join us on the voyage around the Mediterranean. This was either going to make or break us as we hadn't had two full weeks working together in thirty-five years.

I swiped my room key in the lock of my cabin. Maureen's was on another corridor so we stepped into mine, which was a modern and luxurious. We dropped our bags and Maureen jumped and buried her head in the beautiful white linen sheets. We were like kids checking out the room. I was amazed at the shower and called Maureen in to have a look at the bathroom. As I was feeling and admiring the towels, Maureen suddenly called me and I rushed out to see what other exciting things she had found. We were like little girls running around exploring our surroundings. I could see the net drapes blowing in the wind, Maureen had stepped out onto the balcony. As I walked out through the sliding glass door, she turned and said, "We're moving." It was like a scene from a film. I couldn't even feel the ship move and then, in the stillness of the fresh Mediterranean air, we were off, anchors aweigh and we stood peering over the balcony waving goodbye to the Italian coast.

Thinking back now, they must have thought we were mad waving at people on the shore who didn't have a clue who these silly two women were. But we were on a high with happiness and stood on the balcony in silence taking in the views and that stillness of the sea is still a memory I often think back to.

While filming The Nolans Go Cruising

A typical day on the ship would begin with getting up at 6.30-ish. I'd have a shower, order breakfast to my cabin, pop the TV on for background noise as I put on my make-up, then lay clothes on the bed for the day ahead.

Our schedule for the day was arranged the night before by our director and producer. We would take turns with the early interview at about seven thirty a.m. and the next person would take the eight a.m. interview and so on. Then we would all get together and set off for whatever was planned that day, usually splitting into two groups. Two of us with one film crew and two with another. It was usually a different twosome each time.

We sailed to a different city every day and after our early morning interviews we would go ashore and film in whichever city we were in and talk about unusual and hopefully interesting things about that particular city.

Fun behind the scenes filming
The Nolans Go Cruising

Our first stop was in Palermo, then Marseille, then Barcelona. We sailed back to Genoa after one week so we could let passengers off and new people could board. We had the luxury of staying on for a second week. One of our trips in Genoa, which all four of us did together, was to visit Frank Sinatra's favourite restaurant. When we went into the beautiful restaurant, the owner showed us some of Sinatra's memorabilia and showed us around the kitchens, introducing us to the chefs before sitting down to eat.

Now, people that know me, know I have a very particular palate. I have never been great with foreign food and I like ordinary things like egg and chips or a pizza so I was hoping that there would be a margarita or something similar. To my horror it was *pasta*, which was made especially for Sinatra when he visited the restaurant. It's not so much the taste I don't like, it is the texture I hate! I was at a dinner party once and my friend made a beautiful spaghetti Bolognese, and to be polite, I ate the meal but I was almost sick after. So, on this occasion after I had tried it and once again deciding it wasn't for me, as soon as the chef and the owner turned their backs, I passed it to one of my sisters. They found this hilarious, and I still get asked to this day when people meet me, why I don't like pasta!

On our days at sea, we would rehearse for our performances. We would decide who was singing which harmonies and we designated Maureen as the choreographer. As the music started, I began to feel a sense of anxiety. I felt I was going to be behind the other three girls but practice really does make perfect. On my day with Coleen in Marseilles, I had a lovely day and we danced down the marina enjoying life with not a care in the world, while she took me step by step through some of the routine. We really have come a long way since the fall out. I always had a close bond with Coleen as I was the eldest girl and she the youngest, so it was lovely to share that time one on one with her.

While we were on the Med cruising, I had the TV on and was listening to the presenter saying that thirteen people had been infected with the Coronavirus which, at the time, didn't seem like anything to worry about. Italy was beginning to go into lockdown, but we had no idea at the time what this meant. However, over the duration of the cruise we learned that some Italian ports were not allowing ships to dock in fear of the virus spreading. We had arrived in Barcelona at this point, and it fell on Coleen's birthday. We had organised friends and family to send videos while she was away from home so her day could be made even more special. Friends such as Bucks Fizz, Saira Khann, Jeremy Vine and Sir Cliff Richard, to name a few, sent in videos to wish her well on her birthday.

We planned to go for a birthday meal in Barcelona where another surprise was waiting for her: her eldest son Shane had flown over especially. He walked through the door and Coleen almost fell to the floor in shock, it was such a lovely moment. We spent the afternoon in Barcelona before heading back to the ship to prepare for the big performance the following night.

We would have a big day ahead with filming our interviews in the morning, followed by a technical rehearsal and a sound check in the afternoon prior to the big performance.

*Ready to perform I'm In The Mood For Dancing_*

When the time arrived, I stood behind the red velvet curtain that draped across the stage and felt my hand clench round the microphone as a sense of sheer apprehension pulsated through my body. We had come a long way in the ten years since the reunion tour and now here we were, the four of us on stage without Bernie. I got the choreography correct in the end and when we came off stage, I felt as though we were in our heyday again and we all instantly wanted to do it all over again. I loved performing with my sisters and it was so natural to be up there with them again after all those years.

We collected our handbags and danced our way past the bars along the ship laughing and singing our way to our favourite bar to have our final drink with a toast to a wonderful performance.

Since the show aired, I saw the girls talk to the camera and express their regrets about me not being included on the reunion tour, which naturally made me feel good as my pain has been acknowledged.

Chapter 16

The Big C?

2020

We arrived home on such a high after filming the show. It would be a few months before the show was to be aired on TV. When we arrived back in England, to our amazement, the Coronavirus had become a major public concern. Once back in Blackpool, we had to isolate for two weeks so Maureen and I decided to isolate together in Maureen's house and, as Linda lived just across the road, she slept at her house and came over to Maureen's during the day so she wouldn't be alone. So, we had each other's company. It's times like this I love being in a big family. I don't know what I'd have done if I didn't have anyone to chat with or talk to.

Mine and Maureen's kids and grandkids would visit the house and look through the windows and wave at us as though we were captive animals in a zoo and, initially, it was a bit of a laugh. Denise was so good leaving shopping at the doorstep and coming over numerous times a day to check on us, but always from outside. It's hilarious for us, Denise and Linda have houses across the road from Maureen, mine is about five minutes away and our brothers and our kids live within walking distance

When I eventually got home after almost a month away, it was great to be in my own bed and get back to Aunty. At this stage, she was keeping well although her arthritis was very bad. Although she was mobile, she now needed a walker to get around the house. We continued our lives for as long as we could before the first big lockdown came into effect.

Suddenly, I wasn't allowed to visit my daughters and their grandkids; I found this very hard because I spend so much time with them. I can remember at this time how difficult it must have been for people living in flats or apartments where they don't have the luxury of sitting in their back gardens and soaking up the lovely spring sunshine.

Every day was the same in lockdown: I'd get up make Aunty her breakfast. Then, I'd have a cup of tea and a slice of toast and then have my shower. One morning, in early April, I was in the shower when I came across a lump beneath my left breast. When I was in my twenties, I'd had several cysts removed from my breasts so I wasn't unduly worried as I assume it would be another cyst and I went downstairs and continued with my lockdown life of pottering around the house. I was planning on renovating the lounge, so I'd look on my iPad and look at different websites to collect inspiration.

The next day, in the shower once again, I felt the small lump in my left breast. I kept moving different ways to see if it disappeared and hoping it would but, I had to acknowledge that there was definitely a lump there. Even though I didn't really want to know, common sense took over and I called my GP and made an appointment. I saw my doctor the next day and she told me not to worry but she was going to make an appointment at the Breast Care Clinic at Victoria Hospital for me to have a mammogram, just to make sure. I think because I had gone through Breast Cancer before, albeit twenty years previously, I had a feeling what the result of the mammogram would be, and I was right. After several examinations and a meeting with the specialist I was told I had breast cancer. I told my daughters and, although they were very upset, they were so positive and supportive telling me I had beaten it before and I would do it again.

Two days later, Linda told us that her cancer had spread and it was now in her liver.

I was told I would need chemotherapy, an operation to remove the lump and radiotherapy. Linda was also to undergo chemo so she asked the oncologists and head nurse at the oncology unit if we could have it together and, thankfully, they agreed.

This would take place during lockdown so we were not allowed to have anyone with us in the unit, so it was very supportive and helpful to have Linda with me.

I started my treatment in the early morning every three weeks and she would join me for her treatment a couple of hours later. I had four lots of treatment and Linda had one. She used to bring in treats for me like sweets and magazines.

On my second dose of treatment, I had an allergic reaction to one of my chemo drugs. I was just sitting in my chair with the infusion in my arm and all of a sudden I started to feel very strange, with horrendous pain in my back and legs. Linda said my face went from being quite pale to roaring red in about five seconds. I called the medical team and they all rushed over and administered some medication and I was back to normal quite quickly.

One day I said to my oncologist, "Mr Bezecny the chemotherapy is killing me!" to which he swiftly replied, "It'll not be the chemotherapy that will kill you; chemotherapy will save your life." I held onto that for the rest of my treatment and reminded myself on the darkest days that there will be better times ahead.

The next time I had my treatment they gave me the medication before the chemo but once again I had the same reaction, so they took me off that particular chemo and after that I was fine.

During my six months of chemo, Maureen moved into aAunty's house to look after both me and Aunty. She was amazing and did everything for us, shopping, cleaning, cooking, absolutely everything. I don't know what Aunty and I would have done without her, although I know if Maureen hadn't been able to look after me, my daughters definitely would have, but they had work and their children to look after so Maureen was a godsend. Linda moved in with Denise who did exactly the same for her. That's what family is for.

I was quite poorly during my chemo and ended up in hospital for eleven days. Because of Covid I wasn't allowed any visitors but my sister-in-law, Annie, and my ex-brother-in-law, Ian Wilson, who both worked at the hospital, gowned up and came to visit me on separate occasions, which meant a lot. I really had nothing physically wrong with me except a high temperature and palpitations. I was suffering from anxiety, brought on, I think, by the fact I was having chemotherapy during Covid and was told if I contracted Covid, it could be fatal. I received counselling, which helped a lot, and after my chemo finished, I had my operation and then radiotherapy, which all went well. I was told my cancer was no longer there but I would continue to have an infusion of a drug called Zoledronic acid every six months for three years. This is given to try to prevent cancer coming back in the bones. Linda's cancer is treatable but not curable so all we can do is stay positive and hope for the best.

During the summer, our TV show was being aired on TV. We were receiving amazing reviews and we actually broke all records for the network, being the highest rated show when it came to the number of viewers. Dermot and Julian had put together a very strong publicity trail for the series, and we were on the front of countless magazines, newspapers, and featured on breakfast shows and evening shows all around the UK & Ireland.

News started to spread around Blackpool that two of The Nolans were battling cancer. The reason we kept it under wraps for so long was because we didn't want our illness to turn people off the series in fear they thought it would be all about illness and loss, but, in fact, it was the opposite.

When the time was right Linda and I sat down with Dan Wootton, who was the former editor of *The Sun.* Dan would be one of the country's leading showbiz journalists, breaking the Megxit scandal (Harry & Meghan) and countless other major stories. Dan was great with us; he listened and really articulated the story beautifully.

The week before, I met up with Linda at the Village Hotel in Blackpool for the press shots that would be taken. At this stage we were completely bald, we were each coming to the end of our treatment and. Maureen came along to help on the day for a while. I was very tired, so I was delighted to have her around for her support.

The following Monday, Linda and I fronted the Sun with the title reading: *NOLAN SISTERS - Our Double Cancer Battle.* The story went viral with dozens of other newspapers and online editions picking it up. We had a wave of support from fans and other celebrities from all over the world. We were inundated with letters from women and men thanking us for talking about our battle so publicly. I was astonished by the wave of love and support from the public.

Chapter 17

At Home with The Nolans

2021

With the final episode of *The Nolans Go Cruising* airing, the love from the public was electric. It truly made it easier to get me back on the right track. Little by little I got stronger and stronger. On my final chemo session, I rang the bell in the chemo ward, Linda was there to film it and it went viral! Shortly after the end of Linda's and my chemo, we filmed another TV series for Quest Red. This one was called *At Home with The Nolans*.

We filmed around Blackpool and surrounding areas. A few of the other members of the family were involved including our brothers, Denise, my daughters, and Maureen's and my grandchildren.

After five months of gruelling treatment my chemo was over and I was booked in for a lumpectomy later that month. When I went back to meet with the oncologist, Mr Bezecny, I walked into his office and sat in front of his oak desk where my medical records were sitting in a folder. My future was before my eyes. He looked at me and told me that the cancer had disappeared!

Right after my news, I met the girls at the top of Blackpool Tower where I announced to my sisters that I had got the all-clear from my oncologist and the cancer was gone. After the worst few months of my life, this was the reassurance I needed, and I would now be able to move on.

We had a lovely day and filmed scenes at the Opera House Theatre where we had worked many times and where we tried to copy a photograph taken with Amy about thirty-nine years before when she was two. It featured her four aunties when they were working in Torquay, the place where she was born. This time I took the place of Bernie.

We took a lovely trip to the Lakes and stayed in a beautiful house where we watched old family videos that Denise had brought along. It was a real treat to have her with us this time. We really missed her on the cruise and we'd often say, "Oh, Denise would love it here" or, "Denise has been here so many times when she was doing cruise ship circuit".

We showed the public what our family dynamic was really like this time, more in depth, with me filming together with Amy and Alex. I had some lovely scenes with Nevaeh and Vin, and we had some nice scenes in the park with Ryder too.

We visited an owl sanctuary in Grange-over-Sands and went walking with wolves. We actually took two wolves on leads for a small walk around a field. Denise and I were not really too happy about that but the handlers were very experienced and made it all very safe. It was actually an amazing experience.

It was my 70th birthday on 12th November but because of Covid we weren't allowed to have any kind of large gathering as we normally would. So, the TV producer, Alexis, who was so lovely, and had produced our last cruise, suggested that, because we were working together, it would be OK for us to get together as a family.

On the morning of my birthday, we met at Denise's house to do some filming and when I arrived, there were presents and banners and a fabulous book filled with photos and messages from all my family and friends, which our friend Adam, and Denise, had once again, produced. The TV crew also presented me with a beautiful, ornate tree with messages from each of them hanging on the branches.

My best friends arrived, staying in the garden with masks on, and gave me beautiful cards and presents. We then went round to Alex's house and what an amazing surprise I got when the rest of my family were all there and there was a beautiful cake and a huge blow-up pub in the back garden. We sat around Alex and Steve's fire pit eating, drinking and singing. From thinking I wouldn't be able to celebrate my 70th because of Covid, thanks to a fantastic filming crew, and my amazing family and great friends, it turned out to be amazing.

As society reopened in the year 2021, now that science had found a vaccine for the Coronavirus, we were slowly but surely getting ourselves back to normal. Little by little. Linda had her scans returned to her before Christmas 2020. They found that, following the chemo we endured together, it wasn't enough to blast away the tumours in her liver, so it was decided by her oncologist to treat her with a tablet form of chemo. With myself on the road to recovery, I had to be very careful with people I came across in case I caught the virus.

Life continued nicely and I was getting back on my feet and able to enjoy the little things again. We have the most beautiful park in the world in Blackpool. Stanley Park is one place which everyone in our family thinks of as a second home. There is a beautiful art deco café standing proud and looking down the beautiful park where we go, perhaps a little too often.

We were booked for a third television series in the early summer. Initially, we were in two minds about doing this additional cruise as it was only going to be around the British Isles, but we decided to give it a go with Denise joining us this time. Well, for some of it but I'll get to that later.

We set off in a Sprinter van from Blackpool down to Southampton, where we would meet the ship for our two-week staycation—a phrase that was, in my opinion, invented during Covid. As we hadn't travelled for a year or so, none of us had renewed our passports so, when Denise took hers out the day before we were set to leave, to our horror we realised that it was out of date! She picked up the phone and pleaded with the production company. However, their hands were tied as this was a rule of the cruising company. In a frantic hurry, she got in touch with the Irish Embassy to get herself a brand-new passport in the hope of being able to join us.

Maureen, Linda, Coleen and I had no choice but to start the cruise and filming of the show without Denise but, fortunately, she managed to get her new passport and joined us a couple of days later.

It was great being back on the cruise ship and, by now, my hair had started to grow back to a nice length.

As this cruise was around the time of Covid, there was not a lot of things we were allowed to do ashore. We were supposed to visit Belfast and the *Titanic* museum but the ship was not allowed to dock in Belfast so that trip was cancelled.

We did, however, visit Cerne Abbas in Dorset. It depicts a standing nude giant sculpted in chalk. It stands 180 feet and is considered to be an ancient symbol of fertility. In parts it was very, very impressive!

Because of our inability to go ashore in as many places as planned, the things we did had to be on board ship. We were taught a little ballroom dancing which we all thoroughly enjoyed. I had a swimming lesson which was great, although I still can't swim, and then I decided to try and walk around the high ropes on the ship. We have some high ropes in Stanley Park in Blackpool and I thought, if I could do it on the ship, I should be able to do it with my three grandchildren when we got home. I had always been promising them I would do it but as yet had not done so.

It was all arranged for myself and my sisters to do the ropes on the ship and we arrived early one afternoon ready to participate. We all put on the appropriate gear and, as I was the person who had requested it, it was decided I should go first - big mistake. As soon as I walked up the ladder, which I did with immense bravado, and stood on the first platform, I froze in panic. A lovely man, one of the passengers on board, who was waiting to take his turn gave me loads of encouragement and I started to walk. I got as far as the next platform and that was it. I was not going any further. One of the ship's crew working on the ropes came up and asked what I wanted to do, I could go back or forward but I said NO! I wanted to get down but he said that would take an awful lot of time to arrange and that he would hold my hand all the way around whenever possible, so that's what happened. He walked me round holding my hand like a baby. He was fabulously kind and encouraging as were all the staff. There was one area where I had to walk myself just near the end and which I managed to do with great trepidation. When I got to the last platform quite a few people had gathered to watch me including my sisters who were almost in tears because they felt so sorry for me. When I descended the ladder and was back on solid ground I almost burst into tears with relief. I had taken so long going around the ropes that no one else had time to do it, which didn't make me very popular.

While on the ship, we were asked if we would sing for the fellow passengers, so we chose to sing 'I Will Survive' because it was appropriate due to what everyone had just been through with Covid. It was a crowd pleaser and went down a treat with the audience.

Since I had faced some of my fears such as heights and learnt to swim while on the ship, we decided to do some filming at Stanley Park where I had promised my grandchildren I would do the high ropes with them. Having failed miserably on the cruise, I got all geared up and walked with them up to the first platform. Bear in mind this was the lower level, not the highest ones. I could feel my heart beating in my chest and honestly thought I was going to chicken out again, but with my grandchildren's encouragement and my daughters and sisters watching and cheering me on from the ground below, I stepped on to the first platform. I don't know how but I made it all the way round and when I stepped onto the last platform the relief was immense but the applause and cheers from everyone was worth it. Of course, Vinny, Ryder and Nevaeh wanted me to try the highest ropes now, but I said maybe some other time when my heart starts beating normally again.

By this stage, a friend of ours Julian, who is also, coincidentally, a Nolan, phoned me before I went on the cruise ship with my sisters. By now he had started to work as a talent agent in his own right in Ireland working with other singers and broadcasters alike.

He asked me if I would consider taking part in a brand-new reality show called *Celebrity - Pulling with My Parents* for RTE, the Irish national broadcaster. The title of the show does exactly what it says on the tin. They wanted to know if I would be interested in going on the show with my daughter, Amy, who at the time was single and I was offered a very nice fee to take part in the series.

The idea was for me to bring Amy back to Ireland from England and try to find her an Irish hunk. I asked my cousin Angie to come on the show with me to help me on this mission. This was strictly a TV show and we had a lot of fun doing it. In total we spent about three weeks over the summer in two slots filming the show.

When we arrived in Dublin, we checked into a beautiful hotel on Pearse Street. I had the most luxurious room with a balcony peering into Trinity College. In the distance, you could see the glorious sunshine beaming onto the Dublin mountains standing proud over the fair city.

On the first day we went through Amy's Tinder account. To my horror, some of the messages she received were not meant for her mother to read. We fell around, laughing at some of the things the men were saying to her. Honest to God, there was nothing like that when I was her age.

On another day, Angie and I headed for Temple Bar and stopped complete strangers to ask them if they were single and willing to go on a date with Amy.

Relaxing after filming celebrity pulling with my parents. From left; Loraine Cramer (Anne's cousin), Amy (daughter), Anne, cousins Angela Ganly and Valerie Breslin

When we watch the show, we find it utterly comical. Angie is great company, and everyone loves her as she has the ability to make everyone laugh and feel at ease. We were comforted by the fact the production team weren't going to let any stranger go off with Amy as they had security checks behind the people whom we eventually set her up with.

A typical evening after filming would be for us to retire to the hotel bar terrace, have our dinner and enjoy some nice cocktails in the lovely summer evening. We would often be in hysterics as we recalled the day's activities.

While I was in Ireland, Julian had set me up to speak with Breast Cancer, Ireland. This became a charity with which I have become very close over the last few years. A lot of money they raise goes into research.

Front left to right - Roma, Ryder, Middle row - Vinny, Sienna, Ava. Back - Me, Linda - at The Great Pink Run

Linda and I were also asked to become brand ambassador for The Great Pink Run, a massive nationwide event in Ireland. We appeared on many radio and TV shows to promote the event.

****

It was now a year since my second cancer diagnosis, and I decided it was time for me to retire from my day job at The Insolvency Service. I had been there for fifteen years and enjoyed every minute of it. When I first got the job there, it was at a very traumatic time in my life, and it actually saved my life in a way, so it was hard for me to give it up, but I felt the time was right.

It was during Covid so it would have to be a very quiet ending as I couldn't have a big celebration or even say goodbye to my work colleagues. As a result, I went for a quiet meal to a lovely Italian restaurant with Amy, my sisters Denise and Linda (Maureen and Coleen were working), my brother Brian and his wife, Annie, and our friend Dee. There were balloons and banners with 'Happy Retirement' written on and it was a really lovely evening.

Later on, however, my daughters, Amy and Alex, decided they couldn't just let it go by without a larger, more formal acknowledgement, so they arranged for me to go for another meal and, once again, in a lovely Italian restaurant in town with Alex's husband Steve and Amy's then, boyfriend.

When we finished the meal, the girls suggested we go for a drink at a bar at the end of Blackpool's North Pier. I was reluctant at first as it was raining slightly and quite a long walk to the end of the pier, but they persuaded me and I was so glad they did. When we arrived at the bar at the end of the pier, I walked in and was totally surprised and absolutely thrilled to find several of my friends and colleagues and a couple of my extended family waiting for me. They had cordoned off an area of the bar just for us and, once again, there were balloons and banners and we talked and danced the night away.

It truly was a wonderful and unexpected additional celebration of my retirement and a nice way to wrap up the end of 2021.

Alex (left) and Amy at my second retirement party

Chapter 18

Unforgettable

2022

The clocks had just gone back and the evenings were getting darker and colder. I was organising my Christmas decorations when my daughter Alex came round for a cup of tea and helped me lay out all my decorations. She is a complete Christmas anorak!

We had noticed a couple of changes in Aunty Teresa's behaviour. Almost overnight her speech began to get a little slurred and the side of her face had dropped a little. We were concerned that she may have had a minor stroke. She was now eighty-six and had been battling skin cancer for many years.

I took her to the hospital in Blackpool to be assessed and they found no sign of a stroke. However, due to her speech and physical appearance, they decided to carry out an MRI scan to examine the cause of her deterioration. They discovered her cancer had advanced, resulting in a brain tumour. I spoke to the doctor who informed me that Aunty didn't have a lot of time left due to the aggressive nature of the tumour. I didn't tell her straight away as I didn't want to upset her whilst she was in hospital.

The hospital and social services said they would rather she didn't go back home because she had a couple of falls and they wanted to modify the house for her. So, she moved into a lovely care home in Kirkham, about fifteen minutes from Blackpool, but I was the only one allowed to visit her because of Covid. She settled in quite well and I told her it wouldn't be too long until she came home.

At Christmas I asked them if I could take her out for the day to spend it with the family, knowing that it would be her last Christmas. Linda had organised the most wonderful Christmas meal in Lytham Hall. If you're reading this book and don't know where Lytham is, it is the town below Blackpool where Lytham Hall, a Georgian country house dating from the 18th century, stands tall with the most beautiful stately grounds. The house is decked out so beautifully at Christmas with trees and garlands throughout the vast building.

Linda had organised the Christmas meal for our family, and being Irish, every Christmas we have ham or gammon. As they didn't have gammon on the menu, we asked if we could bring our own to which they agreed. So, on Christmas Day we brought a big joint of gammon which we had cooked the night before, and the chef kindly carved it for us. They must have thought we were mad, bringing our own gammon for the chef to carve.

Denise and her partner, Tom, had flown to Los Angeles the week before to spend Christmas with his son and his family, Tom Jnr, who had been living there since he was a child. Coleen also told us she wasn't going to be able to make it as she had made prior commitments with her own family.

It can be difficult to get us all together at any one time but, to our surprise, Coleen arrived on the day, bringing her own family, so we were delighted that she was able to join us.

We sat around the vast Christmas table, the biggest dining table we'd ever seen, singing Christmas carols. I turned to Aunty and smiled to her as we sang, 'Walking in a Winter Wonderland', and took in that special moment. Everyone at the table knew how poorly Aunty was but, as usual at Christmas, she was in festive cheer on the day. By now her speech had got quite bad and we could see she was deteriorating before our eyes so after lunch, which was just wonderful, I took Aunty back to the care home.

In the New Year, we brought Aunty home to her beloved house where she had spent all her married life with her husband Jim. As promised, Social Services had a hospital bed brought in and she had carers in three times a day.

Throughout my life she was a constant, from when I was a little girl to now in my seventies. In many ways she was my best friend, mother, sister and confidante.

On the 3rd of February, Aunty passed away peacefully at home and it was the end of an era. She was the last of our parents' generation. We were all devastated to lose such an immense presence in all our lives. We rallied round for her funeral, organising the service and cremation. The news made it into some of the online papers, which enabled some of our fans to pay their tributes. Many of them remembered Aunty from our shows, coming out of the stage door with her sister, our mum.

Two months after Aunty's funeral, we had an event in the calendar that lifted our spirits. We were to celebrate Denise's 70th birthday. Together, the sisters and brothers and her dear partner, Tom, had organised a fabulous party in Blackpool with friends calling from all around the world to celebrate. Maureen organised a fantastic cake with a photo of Frank Sinatra, Denise's favourite singer, with Denise superimposed next to him and the words 'Young at Heart', one of Sinatra's songs written on it. All my siblings attended and, once again, we had our favourite seven-piece band playing.

Earlier that day Linda had received her chemotherapy, but she was well enough to attend Denise's party. We danced the night away all together. It's hilarious when we're dancing as next to come on would be one of our hits and, immediately we would all get in line and dance to the original choreography from our heyday. My daughters always have their phones out to record these things so when we woke up the next morning it was even funnier to see us dancing after a few glasses of wine!

In our business, every so often you need to rebrand yourself, so I took the opportunity after watching what my grandkids were doing on TikTok and Instagram. While Julian was staying with me for Denise's birthday, I ask him about setting up and organising my social media platforms. He had created them before I did *Pulling with the Parents*, as I needed to have a social media presence to be able to do the show. I decided to become something of a social media influencer. This is a new phrase I've only just learnt! I have been able to connect with people all around the world, who have been fans of The Nolans, reaching people as far as Tokyo and Sydney.

On a handful of occasions, my videos have gone viral. Don't ask me why or how, but I love recording clips from my day-to-day life. I'm now able to post photos and videos on my own and I get a real buzz from it.

Chapter 19

That's Amore

We have had 'three weddings and a funeral' this year, with a fourth wedding to come in December.

The first wedding was in January and was my nephew and godson, Tommy, and his beautiful fiancée, Millie. Their wedding service was in a beautiful little church in Millie's home town with the reception and evening party just ten minutes away in gorgeous Larkspur Lodge, Knutsford. The bride looked absolutely beautiful, and the groom didn't look too bad either. The weather was a little bit chilly but sunny. It was a beautiful wedding, and we all had a wonderful time.

The second wedding was in July and it was that of my nephew, Shane, and his beautiful fiancée, Maddi. Their wedding service and reception was at Rushton Hall in Kettering, halfway between Shane and Maddi's family homes. It was a scorching hot day and, once again, the bride looked beautiful, and the groom didn't look too bad either. Once again, we all had a fabulous time.

The third wedding was in August and was that of my nephew, Danny, and his beautiful fiancée, Maddie. It was in beautiful Sorrento so we decided to make it a little holiday while attending the wedding. Amy, Ryder and I, together with most of the guests, arrived a few days before the wedding. We visited some lovely restaurants with amazing sea views. Myself, Amy, Ryder, Alex and Steve, Vinny and Nevaeh and my brother Brian and his wife Annie, hired a little yacht with a skipper and sailed to Capri. We stopped at an appropriate spot and everyone went swimming in the sea except Brian and I, of course. When we got to Capri, we docked and then dined at a lovely restaurant right by the sea.

The wedding service and reception was held in a gorgeous villa just outside Sorrento with spectacular views. The bride again looked stunning and the groom not too bad either. Once again, the wedding was amazing and we all had a fabulous time.

The day after the wedding Amy, Ryder and I went by cab to Positano about a twenty-minute drive from Sorrento. It was a beautiful day and we had decided to get the ferry back to Sorrento at the end of the day. The taxi left us right at the top of Positano and we had a very long walk down steep steps to the harbour.

We were having lunch at a lovely harbourside restaurant when the heavens opened with the most torrential rain I had ever seen, even in England. We just weren't dressed for that kind of weather and had no raincoats or umbrellas, not even a jacket. It was also thundering very loudly so we decided it wouldn't be a good idea to go back to Sorrento by ferry and decided to get a taxi. To our horror we were told we would have to go back up to the top to get a cab so after buying three umbrellas, we started our climb back up the mountain of steps. By the time we got to the top, we were all drenched but still in good spirits. A lovely man in a little café called a cab for us and let us shelter inside the café. The cab came about fifteen minutes later, and we arrived back in Sorrento tired and wet but still happy that we'd made the trip to Positano. Altogether, we had a wonderful time in Italy and I would certainly like to go back.

A couple of weeks after returning home I was asked to support The Great Pink Run, a charity for Breast Cancer Research in Dublin. I had been made an ambassador for the charity a year before when I did a photoshoot with Linda and my grandchildren and great-nieces wearing their logo on our tee shirts. I was delighted to accept and everything was arranged by Julian who was now my manager. He arranged to have me flown to Dublin, with Amy and my friend Billy to stay at the gorgeous Trinity City hotel, where I had stayed when I filmed the TV show with Amy.

An hour after my arrival in Dublin, I filmed the *Six o'Clock Show* for Virgin Media to advertise the Charity Run. We had a table booked in a beautiful restaurant called Sophie's Rooftop and, after having a glass too many, I began singing 'La Vie en Rose' to the French waiter. We all fell around laughing and singing as we strolled back to the hotel down Grafton Street.

The next day, which was Saturday, I did a photoshoot for this book cover and was looked after like royalty by Grace Cahill who organised the most wonderful hair treatment in Sugar Brown Hair Salon on South William Street. A 'smart end of town' salon, where I had a back massage as my hair was being washed. Yes, a back massage! Grace was fantastic on the day. I was thinking a lot about the following day where I was to sing in front of 4000 people: something I hadn't done in a while.

On Sunday I arrived at Leopardstown racecourse for the charity run. The lovely Nicky and Aising from Breast Cancer Ireland met us. I wasn't physically doing the run, but I sang a couple of song before it actually started. I sang 'Footloose' from the show of the same name and then gave a speech about the way in which I had dealt with breast cancer before finishing off my stint on stage with 'I'm In The Mood for Dancing'.

I had a wave of ladies come up to me after the performance some to just ask for a photo and others to just plainly thank me for speaking out and supporting the cause. It was so moving being there. I watched from the windows of the changing area I had been given as a group of pink attired runners started their run. Shortly after, we packed up our things and made our way back to England.

The charity made about half a million euros that day and it was so emotional.

I started this book almost five years ago and after deciding to pull it out of that drawer in the summer of 2022, I felt now was the right time to finish it and tell my last story.

I suppose I've come full circle as I haven't had the easiest times over the last fifteen years or so, but as I write this book today, I count my blessings.

The argument with my sisters happened and today we see each other almost on a daily basis. Linda has moved back into her home after having a beautiful renovation done. Maureen is still a very popular fixture on the musical circuit and is hoping to spend more time with her son Danny and his wife Maddison. Denise and Tom live a lovely life these days, splitting time between London and Blackpool and Denise as usual, still running around with her camcorder! Coleen is still going from strength to strength with her wonderfully successful TV career while enjoying life on her little farm. Brian & Tommy are still working their 9-5 jobs and we see them all the time. My two wonderful daughters are living their own independent lives raising my gorgeous grandchildren, Vinny, Ryder & Nevaeh, whom I live for. At the end of the day, family is everything.

I have worked in some of the finest musical venues, worked with my hero Frank Sinatra and been a part of a record-breaking TV series *The Nolans Go Cruising.* I get to do the things I like when I like and how I like. If Julian gets me a job that doesn't excite me, I politely decline, otherwise I jump at the opportunity. Now I think it's time for me to continue to enjoy my wonderful and blessed life.

Chapter 20

Last Chapter!

2023

After auntie's funeral I found it very hard to stay in her house on my own. I was 72 years of age and had never lived on my own at any time in my life. I moved out of the family home when I met and married Brian in my 20's and after we divorced, I moved in with auntie. All of a sudden
I was alone in aunty's house, which was too big for one person. Fortunately, my wonderful sister Maureen stayed with me and my fabulous friend and ex manager Billy Walker stayed whenever he was singing in Blackpool.

Eventually though I decided to sell the house and move into something smaller. I would spend months looking at different properties in the Blackpool area, usually roping in my sister Maureen or my best friend Jacqui to come and have a look with me and we must have viewed every type of house from apartments on the seafront with a balcony view to bungalows close to the park. Eventually, I found a brand new house on a lovely little new housing estate which was perfect for me. I have a spare room for the grandkids or any friends that may be coming to visit. It was a bittersweet moment leaving aunty's house and handing over the keys. I stood in the empty lounge to the front of the house, at this time all the furniture had been removed and on its way to my new house. The house had seen a lot of good times for me; it was the place where I lived when all my grandchildren were born, including when Alex and Steve brought Vinny home from the hospital too. It's also the house where I endured the side effects of my chemotherapy when I had cancer in 2020. My new house is wonderful, I have a lovely modern kitchen on the ground floor with a spacious cosy lounge looking onto my back garden and I've made friends with some lovely neighbours.

It was May 20th and a beautiful, sunny day in Blackpool with not a cloud in the sky. I was preparing to launch my second book with a book signing at Waterstones in Blackpool. Julian my agent, had flown over from Ireland where he lived so that he could coordinate all the things that come along with launching and promoting a book. We took a cab into Blackpool town centre and pulled up outside Waterstones bookstore at 11:00 am where there was a queue waiting for my arrival to attend my book signing. I had laughingly said to Julian in the car , 'I bet you we will turn up and there will be nobody there', but I needn't have worried as familiar faces from our heyday were standing in the queue with their now grown-up children and some friends came along to congratulate me and support my book. The local paparazzi arrived and took shots of me in the store and a lovely lady in the shop mentioned to me that people started arriving 3 hours earlier! We have been so fortunate in having the best fans, some of them have been with us for over 60 years when the family act toured the northern working men's clubs.

Later that evening, I had a bit of a doo at the Beach House, a luxurious beach bar at the footsteps of the Blackpool tower peering out to the Irish Sea. I had invited all my family and all of my friends down to toast and celebrate the book. We had a great night and danced the night away to live music.

The following day we set off for London for the official book promo tour that Julian had coordinated. My first interview was for ITV's *This Morning.* I learned the night before the show that the regular hosts Philip Scofield and Holly Willoughby would not be hosting the show due to extenuating circumstances. I wasn't quite sure what the atmosphere would be like and who the two new hosts would be!

When I arrived at the studio, a lovely young chap met us and brought us into hair and make-up to get me camera ready, nobody wanted to mention what was happening in the news regarding *This Morning.* On the show that day were Dermot O'Leary and Alison Hammond and as I came into the studio and took my place on the sofa, I had a brief chat with the pair during the commercial break and was greeted by a wonderful surprise when my baby sister Coleen came into the studio to say hi and to hug me good luck. Dermot and Alison were very kind and lovely, they made me feel relaxed and very welcome. After that I was whisked off for a day of radio interviews and more book promos, I stayed in London for 3 days promoting my book and did *The Jeremy Vine Show* before hopping on a plane to Ireland for the Irish leg of publicity.

Once again, I did some TV and radio, including The Six O'clock show and the same scenario as all the TV and radio I did, everyone was so lovely. While in Ireland I was invited to the prestigious VIP Style Awards at a beautiful venue in Dublin. VIP magazine has always been so kind to me . When I got back to England after the book promo I was very tired but felt great, the book went down well with readers and got great reviews!

It wasn't too much longer before I was headed back to the land of my birth., I had been booked to perform at Ireland's biggest throwback festival, the 'Forever Young Festival' and my daughter Amy came with me for support. If you have read my last book you may recall an incident when we were promoting one of our albums as The Nolans, we were flown every weekend by a small private jet from Blackpool, where we were doing a summer season to a different major city in Great Britain, on our return to Blackpool, just as we were about to land, one of the plane's engines stopped. I was sitting next to the pilot and he assured me the plane was very capable of landing with one engine which thankfully it did. When we touched down there was a crusade of fire engines and ambulances on hand in case there was a tragedy, thankfully they were not needed but we were all shaken from it.

Since then I have had a fear of flying and when there is an option, I like to take the ferry, especially in the summertime. You might assume it would be plane sailing, but this was far from the case. The sea was very rough, the worst I had ever experienced, people were throwing up all over the place as the ship rocked from side to side for the 3 hours during the crossing. I felt like I was on the waltzers at the Pleasure Beach! I was fine, but poor Amy who has a phobia of vomiting really struggled the whole time on the ship, although she never actually got sick but before we knew it we had arrived in Dublin.

I was booked the following morning to appear on Ireland AM to promote the festival, interviewing me was Big Brother winner Brian Dowling who I had met before at the VIP style awards. He was lovely to me and mentioned that he once worked with Bernie and recalled lovely memories, so it was lovely to see him again. Also interviewing me was Katja Mia, the pair were great and conducted a great interview.

Julian had organised a special surprise for me in the city centre, we arrived at the 5-star Morrison Hotel, where the manager brought us to a hotel room, where they had decorated the wall with the lyrics to "I'm In The Mood for Dancing" I couldn't believe it, each room in the hotel is dedicated to an Irish artist and they had decided to honour The Nolans. Upon my arrival, we had a beautiful lunch in the hotel, the whole experience was an honour and so exciting to see.

One of the best things I've ever done was the outdoor 80's pop festival, 'Forever Young'. I had never done a pop festival before, not even with my sisters, so I was extremely nervous but once I got on stage and started singing I was fine. The audience was amazing especially when I announced that it was my first pop festival at age 72 so that helped overcome my nerves. I met some fabulous icons from the 80's including Billy Ocean who actually co-wrote one of our hits, "Whose Gonna Rock You". We actually sang a couple of lines together in the green room after the show. I also met Pete Cox from 'Go West' who had recorded a song with my sister Bernie a few years previously and Tony Hadley the frontman from Spandau Ballet. They were all so fabulous. It was another wonderful memory to add to all the other memories made in an amazing career both on my own and with my sisters.

My life now is still very busy, mostly taken up with my family. I see my daughters and their families almost every day. Spend every weekend watching my grandchildren playing football, including my granddaughter Nevaeh who I think will be a future 'Lioness'. I see my sisters every week when we go out for lunch or dinner or walks on the beach or in the countryside. I also still see my best friends every week and occasionally meet with my other friends from school each month. I am still ready to do anything interesting that might come up connected with my career. Life is wonderful and I am blessed.

Postscript

This is the second book I have written, and it was just as enjoyable as writing the first. It brought back some wonderful memories and some not so good, but that is what life is about.

In both my books, I decided I wanted to write about my life, all my life, not just the good parts. The hard parts have made me stronger and made me appreciate the good parts even more.

I have had a fortunate life, a wonderful husband, albeit that our marriage only lasted twenty-five years but it was great while we were together. We have two amazing daughters, who are, and always will be, my life from the moment they were born and a fabulous son-in-law. Furthermore, I have three fantastic grandchildren who continue to make my life worthwhile.

I have wonderful sisters and two wonderful brothers and fabulous cousins. Even though we went through a bad patch, I think it made us realise nothing is more important than family. I also have some amazing friends who have become part of the family. In addition, I was fortunate enough to have a wonderful career where I met people I might never have met otherwise and taken me to places I might never have visited.

Altogether, it's been a truly wonderful life and I am so lucky to have lived it.

Back: Amy & Ryder
Front: Vinny, Anne, Nevaeh & Alex

Pressman
House

Printed in Great Britain
by Amazon